IN THE NAZI ERA

IN THE NAZI ERA

BY

SIR LEWIS NAMIER, F.B.A.
PROFESSOR OF MODERN HISTORY IN THE
UNIVERSITY OF MANCHESTER
HON. FELLOW OF BALLIOL COLLEGE, OXFORD

LONDON
MACMILLAN & CO. LTD
1952

PRINTED IN GREAT BRITAIN

PREFACE

THE present volume is a continuation of my work on pre-war diplomacy, of which the first two instalments appeared in *Diplomatic Prelude, 1938–1939*, and in *Europe in Decay, 1936–1940*; it is probably also the last instalment, at least for some time to come. During the past ten years I devoted a good part of my leisure to this work but I always meant ultimately to return to my own chosen field of British Parliamentary history. In February 1951, H.M. Government announced their decision to give financial support to a History of Parliament; and having been put in charge of the modern period, covering the 18th and 19th centuries, I must eschew other work, at least till my main task within the field assigned to me is completed. I have, therefore, for the time being, to take leave of pre-war diplomatic history and my readers in that province.

I have to thank the editors and owners of *The Times Literary Supplement*, *History Today*, *The Listener*, the *Manchester Guardian*, and the *National Review* for permission to reprint essays, or parts of essays, which appeared in their columns.

L. B. N.

60 THE GRAMPIANS
LONDON, W.6
March 21, 1952

[illegible] The Grampians,
London, W.6.
March [illegible]

CONTENTS

PART I

MEN WHO SERVED HITLER

PART II

SURRENDER TO DANGER

PART I

MEN WHO SERVED HITLER

"MISSED OPPORTUNITIES"

The Gravamen of German Memoirs

Were opportunities missed by the Allies in their treatment of Germany? The question clearly does not refer to those for stopping German rearmament and Hitler's frenzied career — that these were missed no one can doubt. But were opportunities missed during the Weimar period for reintegrating a democratic Germany into the European comity of nations, or, later on, for active co-operation with anti-Nazi elements in Germany?

There is now in Allied hands an amount of material for a history of those years such as historians never had for any previous period; and it will be an irreparable loss if any of the captured German archives are returned without having been microfilmed. Some of the material has by now been rendered accessible, and the minutes and documentation of the various Nuremberg trials would alone form a small library. Still, it will take many years and the work of many scholars before even the most important material has been printed and digested; and even then such publications will reach only a very narrow circle of readers. But long before well-founded judgments percolate to a wider public, tenets and slogans, based on insufficient or deliberately twisted evidence, may strike root — as happened with German propaganda after the First World War.

The first thing which will reach that wider public are one-volume memoirs and romanticized biographies. These the Germans are producing by the dozen: some write them to furbish up tarnished reputations; others to make money; and all alike to make out a case for the German nation. Most of these writers make at best a perfunctory reference to the unbelievable crimes committed by a régime which, as long as it was successful, had the enthusiastic support of the German nation. How many people will read the evidence of those crimes carefully examined and sifted by men of undoubted integrity and standing? In countries which have not experienced German occupation, to every student who will examine these unspeakably painful and shameful records there will be hundreds of readers who will derive their impression of that period in Germany largely from German memoirs.

The first Germans to publish their memoirs are men who served Hitler but who now try to prove that in reality they opposed or even sabotaged him, or that at least they were out of sympathy and out of favour with the Nazi régime. There are the memoirs of Schacht, Hitler's financial wizard; Weizsäcker, State Secretary in the German Foreign Office, 1938–1943; Dirksen, Ambassador to Moscow, Tokyo, and London; Erich Kordt, for nearly seven years Ribbentrop's secretary; Schmidt, official interpreter of the German Foreign Office and of Hitler; Meissner, *chef de cabinet* to the Socialist President Ebert, to Hindenburg, and to Hitler; and by many other minor servants of the régime whose makers and leaders are practically all dead.

The factual material in these books is mostly of very small value: some of the writers supply a selective or embellished rehash of evidence which they gave at Nuremberg, now without having to face cross-examination; others dish up selections from their dispatches or memoranda; some pad their books with second-hand material which they produce as if it was derived from their own personal knowledge and experience; still others seem to give a free rein to their imagination; and what seems most odd is how many of these former members of the German Civil Service, with its reputation for meticulous accuracy, are staggeringly inaccurate even where no political purpose enters into the matter. Thus Dirksen muddles up his dates and constructs impossible time-tables; Schmidt seems not to have studied even his own printed minutes; and after Kordt had in his first book printed an imaginary text of Mussolini's letter to Hitler, of August 25, 1939,[1] others have copied it from him without noticing that he himself dropped it in his second edition: it reappears in Schmidt,[2] even in the English edition;[3] it appears again in the recently published memoirs of Peter Kleist;[4] in short, it has become a fixture in German historical literature. The genuine text of the letter was published in Italy in 1946,[5] before Kordt ever printed his concoction, and by the American State Department in 1948,[6] without either having any effect on such German productions. Serious students would be well-advised to treat this mushroom growth of memoirs with the utmost reserve, and readers had best accept nothing from them unless confirmed by some independent and more scholarly authority.

These memoirs are of value mainly as illustrating the minds and characters of their authors, and certain trends in the formation of German myths. Mussolini once said about the Germans that they are dangerous because they dream collectively. More than that: they remember collectively; they invent collectively; they are unsurpassed in mental gregariousness. Whenever German memoirs touch on the pre-1914 period, they almost invariably assert, as is done by Weizsäcker, that while German policy was clumsy, that of the *Entente* was set

[1] *Wahn und Wirklichkeit* (1947), pages 193-4.
[2] *Statist auf diplomatischer Bühne 1923–45* (1949), pages 452-3.
[3] *Hitler's Interpreter* (1951), pages 145-6.
[4] *Zwischen Hitler und Stalin, 1939–1945* (1950), page 69.
[5] *Hitler e Mussolini. Lettere e Documenti*, pages 10-11.
[6] *Nazi-Soviet Relations*, pages 82-3.

on war; and long-disproved lies about Sir Edward Grey are dished up afresh. When German writers reach the Paris Peace Conference and the Treaty of Versailles, vituperation becomes well-nigh automatic. Men like Weizsäcker or Erich Kordt must know about the long deliberations and struggles within the Allied delegations, and between them, over the peace terms for Germany; how, for instance, Lloyd George supported by Philip Kerr (the later Lord Lothian) and by Headlam-Morley brought about a revision of these terms against the judgment of the foremost Foreign Office experts, Eyre Crowe and William Tyrrell, hoping that such revision would render them acceptable to fair-minded Germans. But this does not prevent Weizsäcker from asserting that it was the deliberate aim of the Versailles Treaty to create permanent discord between Germany and Poland. Or again, Erich Kordt, having described how, in November 1938, Ribbentrop and Ciano, when called upon to make a frontier award between Czechoslovakia and Hungary, impromptu drew it with thick coloured pencils, remarks: " More frivolous could not have been even the treatment of frontiers at Versailles ". But all this is merely a fitting prelude to the further German indictment of the Allies.

That indictment affirms that the Allies, and not the Germans, are to blame for what has happened in the last thirty years. First it asserts that the Allies, by conceding too little and too late, caused the downfall of the peace-loving Weimar Republic; next, that good and true men in the German Army and Foreign Office were plotting against Hitler in September 1938, and were about to overthrow him when Neville Chamberlain, though warned by them to take a strong line with Hitler, saved him by the ill-timed visits to Berchtesgaden and Munich; and lastly, that Mr. Churchill and President Roosevelt, by insisting on Germany's unconditional surrender, unnecessarily prolonged the war and destroyed Germany as a bulwark against Soviet Russia.

How much truth is there in these assertions? Undoubtedly, if after the First World War the Western Powers had promptly evacuated the occupied zones of Germany, written off reparations, and admitted Germany to equality in armament, the Germans would have felt that a measure of atonement had been made for the crime of defeating them — or for their having been, according to Hitler, fooled into throwing away their arms by chatter about President Wilson's Fourteen Points. That financial restitution and military security for the future were France's due is not acknowledged — Weizsäcker condemns even Locarno as too high a price paid for Germany's readmission to the European comity. But anyhow, for the Germans the immediate problem was not in the West but in the East. Although about 80 per cent of the autochthonous population in the territories ceded by them to Poland were Polish, not one responsible German statesman or general of the Weimar period would have accepted those frontiers as final. Dirksen says that the Germans expected the Corridor, Upper Silesia, and the greater part of Posnania to be restored to them; speaks approvingly of the Rapallo Treaty, concluded in 1922 with the Bolsheviks on an anti-Polish basis; relates how that proud Junker, Count Brockdorff-Rantzau, in 1928, on his death-bed wrote a farewell letter to Chicherin and Litvinov exhorting them to continue the tradition of German-Russian friendship; and describes the co-operation between the Reichswehr and Soviet Russia, destroyed, to Dirksen's unfeigned regret, by Hitler.[1] Weizsäcker's most pleasing memories of his work at Geneva seem to be of German collaboration with the Russians, to which spice was added by the annoyance that, according to him, it caused Lord Cecil; nor does Weizsäcker hide the

[1] See below, pages 47-53.

satisfaction he felt at Hitler entering into negotiations with Stalin in 1939;[1] and from authoritative documents it is known how both Halder and Weizsäcker, in 1940 and 1941, tried to convince Hitler that possible Anglo-Russian co-operation should be prevented by cessions to Russia at the expense of Britain rather than by attacking Russia. Examples of that wish for co-operation with Russia, whatever her régime, can be multiplied almost indefinitely — at its root was an old Prussian tradition, hostility against Poland, and the hope for a common domination of Europe. Thus General von Seeckt, Chief of the Reichswehr from 1920 to 1926, and as such one of the most powerful men in Weimar Germany, wrote in July 1922, in a memorandum[2] not for some fellow-Junkers but for the Catholic Chancellor, Wirth, and the Socialist President, Ebert, men representing the core of the Weimar democracy:

> Poland's existence is intolerable, and incompatible with the vital needs of Germany. She must disappear, and disappear she will through her own inner weakness and through Russia's action — with our help. . . . Poland is even more intolerable to Russia than to us; no Russia can agree to her existence. With Poland falls one of the main pillars of the Versailles Treaty, namely the predominance of France. To reach that goal, must be one of the fixed aims of German policy, because that goal is attainable. But it can be attained only through Russia or with her help.

Friendship with the West would have made no change in Germany's program; in fact, a condition of that friendship was a free hand for Germany in the East: the distinction made at Locarno between her western and her eastern frontiers was significant. But if Germany, in

[1] See below, pages 78-9.

[2] Published in the Berlin monthly, *Der Monat*, November 1948: "Der Seeckt-Plan".

collaboration with Russia, had re-established her position in Eastern and South-Eastern Europe, how long would she have remained moderate in the West or over colonies? After Sadowa came Sedan; after Munich, a second Sedan. German apologias, when read critically, offer surprising admissions.

And now for the story of the frustrated plots against Hitler. Weizsäcker said in evidence at his trial: [1]

> Twice we started plans against Hitler. . . . The first plan failed because when it was supposed to be put into practice, the news came that Neville Chamberlain had agreed to go to see Hitler at Berchtesgaden, and thus cut the ground under our feet. The second plan became invalid because, on the 27th . . . the world heard that a Four-Power Conference would take place the next day in Munich.

How very unfortunate! But what was the basis of that conspiracy which evaporated in the heat of Hitler's successes? Very simple: these generals and diplomatists could not believe that the Western Powers would abandon Czechoslovakia, as Hitler maintained they would; and were convinced that Germany would suffer defeat in a major war. They therefore wanted to stop Hitler from rashly provoking it, instead of patiently working for what Weizsäcker called with approval a "chemical dissolution" of Czechoslovakia: a difference in tactics rather than in aims or morals. The moment the Western Powers gave way, the reason for opposing Hitler was gone. But had they not given way, would there have been a *coup* against Hitler? And would it have succeeded? General Halder, according to his own testimony, was the man who had "to fix the date when it should take place"; [2] and about him, Fabian von Schlabrendorff, one of the

[1] June 15, 1948, page 8717.

[2] *Nazi Conspiracy and Aggression*, U.S. Government Printing Office (1948), Supplement B, page 1552.

few surviving genuine conspirators, writes:[1] "As I heard from Oster, Halder, too, was very nearly determined".[2] Similarly Schacht, then in close touch with Halder, writes:[3] "Halder seems to have been relatively determined". With leaders nearly or relatively determined, conspiracies do not succeed against a Hitler or a Gestapo — and this explains a good deal also of the failure of July 20, 1944. Weizsäcker writes about the period after Munich:[4]

> It was clear that Hitler gambled recklessly with Germany's fate and future, that he should not have been suffered to continue doing so, and that the power should somehow have been taken from him. . . . Why then was the step, prevented by Chamberlain's visits in September 1938, left unrepeated in the Spring and Summer of 1939? My notes say nothing about it. . . . I have to rely on my memory for an answer why the important six months preceding the outbreak of war passed without action against Hitler. Was it for lack of a suitable man? Not everyone is cut out for the part of a Brutus, and not every time suits a Brutus. The German by nature is ill-fitted for a revolutionary.

And he concludes: "Much was discussed, but no attempt was made to act. . . ." And Erich Kordt thus winds up a tale full of melodrama: "It was not an accident, nor fate, but our own insufficiency which got us where we now stand".[5]

Would it not therefore be more decent to bury altogether the story of Chamberlain's fatal intervention?

And now for the German thesis about unconditional surrender as against a negotiated peace of cordial understanding: what were the terms on which the "good

[1] *Offiziere gegen Hitler* (1946), page 31.
[2] General Oster was an assistant of Admiral Canaris.
[3] *Abrechnung mit Hitler* (1948), page 22.
[4] *Erinnerungen* (1950), pages 224-6.
[5] See below, pages 96-7.

Germans " were prepared to negotiate while still able to put forward conditions? Erich Kordt quotes from his own memorandum of October 1939, which, he says, received the approval of the military leaders: " peace with honour " should have left Germany the Munich frontiers; reconnected East Prussia with the Reich; and retroceded to it the industrial area in Upper Silesia.[1] And here is another set of territorial terms put forward by von Hassel and his friends in February 1940 (quoted from Hassel's own English version):[2]

> IV. The purpose of a peace treaty ought to be a permanent pacification and re-establishment of Europe on a solid base and a security against a renewal of warlike tendencies.
>
> V. Condition, necessary for this result, is to leave the union of Austria and the Sudeten with the Reich out of any discussion. In the same way there would be excluded a renewed discussion of occidental frontier-questions of the Reich. On the other hand, the German-Polish frontier will have to be more or less identical with the German frontier of 1914.

In other words, the Hitler profits were to be preserved unimpaired.

Would the " good Germans " have insisted on some such terms in 1943 or '44 or '45? It depends on the chances which a negotiation would have offered them. The need of defeating Germany decisively, and of thus preventing the rise of a new legend about her not having been defeated but cheated into surrender, was only one element in the situation. What mattered most was not to reproduce the situation which, at the Congress of Vienna, enabled Talleyrand to manœuvre between the Powers of the victorious Coalition and finish as the ally of Great Britain and Austria against Russia and Prussia. If in 1919 there was unwillingness to negotiate with the

[1] See below, pages 100-101.

[2] *The von Hassel Diaries* (1948), pages 110-11.

Germans about the peace terms, the reason for it lay not in a desire to dictate, but in an attempt to avoid the dangers inherent in re-discussing terms laboriously agreed upon between a number of allies. Experience has shown by now what it would have meant to seek agreement with Soviet Russia on terms to be presented to the Germans. But if differences had appeared between the Western Allies and Russia, there can hardly be a doubt which side would have been best able to buy the friendship and co-operation of the Germans. Soviet Russia could have offered them the frontiers of the Ribbentrop–Molotov Treaty of August 1939, or Germany's old eastern frontier of 1914; whereas the Western Allies could hardly have offered them even the frontier of the Versailles Treaty, especially if Poland was reduced in the East to the Curzon Line. However justified that line is ethnically, the Poles could not have been asked by their Western Allies to accept it without compensation, at the very least in Danzig and Upper Silesia: that is, without a better access to the sea and a recovery of the Polish-speaking districts lost by Poland in the Silesian plebiscite. In short, negotiations with the Germans would not have established a German bulwark against Russia, but would have re-established a Russian-German alliance, and resulted in their common domination of the Continent under Soviet leadership.

THE GERMAN ARMY AND HITLER

Exercitus facit imperatorem — who was it that made Hitler a dictator? The S.A. and S.S.? Or was it the Reichswehr who, by their connivance, enabled him to grip and hold a monstrous plenitude of power such as no German ruler had wielded before him? And as things developed, were they not entitled, or even in duty bound, to stop him in his frenzied course? They alone retained the means with which to attempt it and they still claimed moral leadership of the nation. Yet apparently it was not till early in 1938 that some at least of the Army chiefs came to face the problem; they began to stir uneasily and to plot, but action did not result till after crimes and ruin on the most gigantic scale had been accomplished; and then it proved ineffective. Now the inquest has started;[1] and that inquest will have to go deep and far, seeing the unique position which the Army had long held, and still aspired to, in German national life. " Our people in their *pietas* towards the Army (*unser militärfrommes Volk*)", wrote General Beck, C.G.S., in January 1937, " place a confidence in the Wehrmacht which hardly knows limits. . . . To them the Wehrmacht is both people and State. . . ." And some six years earlier, General Groener, then Reichswehr Minister, described the Army as " the first servant of the State . . . the rock

[1] Gordon A. Craig, " Reichswehr and National Socialism: The Policy of Wilhelm Groener, 1928–1932 "; *Political Science Quarterly*, vol. lxiii, no. 2, June 1948; New York. Friedrich Hossbach: *Zwischen Wehrmacht und Hitler, 1934–1938.* Wolfenbütteler Verlagsanstalt. 1949. Wolfgang Foerster: *Ein General kämpft gegen den Krieg. Aus den nachgelassenen Papieren des Generalstabchefs Ludwig Beck.* Münchener Dom-Verlag, 1949.

upon which the State is built"; moreover, as a power protecting and educating the people. Indeed, for more than a century the *Volksheer*, recruited by universal service, had been the great educational agency which, for good and evil, formed the ethos of the German people — their *Sittlichkeit* or *mœurs*; and the idea and practice of "service" (completely alien to Hitler's Austrian mind) were mighty factors in the Prussianizing of Germany.

In the barren Baltic plain, devoid of a cultural past, arose the Prussian State, the one potent, formative synthesis in German political history. Its original founders were the Teutonic Knights, a semi-monastic military order: cruel conquerors and harsh masters. Austerity, discipline, and self-denial remained basic elements in the Prussian tradition; they made its strength and invested it with a semblance of greatness — a hollow greatness; for these virtues, military in origin and neither humane nor humanizing, were uncorrelated to a moral cause and did not aim at a higher way of life. The Army was not an instrument but *Selbstzweck*, its own purpose; service was unquestioning, and self-denial and self-sacrifice were their own justification. That the aim justifies the means is an all-too-human doctrine formulated by Latins; but downright inhuman is the implied belief of the German introvert that the means can sanctify the aim. Moreover, renunciation of control over the joint purpose has for corollary a restriction of individual responsibility; this in the aggregate field ceases to be human and becomes functional, and extends no farther than the task with which the man is charged — things done outside its range he may deplore, but need not react against. So long as Nazi abominations were committed outside the range of the Army's immediate responsibility, even the best among its chiefs did not feel it incumbent upon them to intervene or to refuse further service to the régime, but when Hitler's encroachments resulted in misdirection within their own province (or if he offended against their narrow, rigid "code of honour") they reacted — only to find that they could not carry the rest with them.

> The [Nazi] régime had undoubtedly the support of a majority of the nation [writes General Hossbach]. Should, or could, the generals have acted against the majority opinion at a time when within the province which was most particularly theirs, the building of the *Wehrmacht*, the inner structure of their work could, by and large, be safeguarded against encroachments by the Party, when the *Wehrmacht* was achieving its development alongside the Party or often against it, and when the growing *Volk* community was gaining over the German working masses to the national idea. . . ?

Even in the present inquest, as conducted by Germans, the question of the Army's responsibility is made to turn on the catastrophe of defeat and not on how a body which claimed to stand for a higher tradition and a Christian morality, and which had it in its power to act, could witness, unmoved, things equally abominable whether the outcome was victory or defeat.

It takes an effort to readjust oneself to the peculiar repressions and blanks in German thought. In April 1919, Groener, perhaps the most intelligent and upright among the generals, emphasized in the German Cabinet

> the importance of the army as a centre for the physical and moral education of German youth . . . the indispensable agency for inculcating . . . those virtues of order, discipline, and service which were essential to healthy State life. His official and private attempts to persuade the Allies to admit the principle of universal service in the military terms of the treaty were influenced in part by his knowledge that, without such concession, the educative rôle of the army would be seriously handicapped.

Groener was right. The German, deprived of his *Volksheer*, turned to para-military bodies imbued with the militarism of political gangsters; still, it required a German to suppose that the Allies would equate the Reichswehr with the Salvation Army and for reasons of social and political hygiene allow Germany to re-create her military power. And now German generals, or their spokesmen, argue that war did not enter into the plans and calculations of those who secretly rearmed under Weimar, and who next favoured Hitler because of the increased facilities which they could expect from him.

> Before 1938–1939 [wrote General von Blomberg in his affidavit at Nuremberg] the German generals were not opposed to Hitler. There was no reason to oppose Hitler since he produced the results which they desired.

Wolfgang Foerster, in his book on General Beck, calls it "incomparable cynicism" in Hitler to have declared: "In principle I did not raise the Wehrmacht in order not to fight. All along I was determined to fight. Sooner or later I meant to solve the problem." As France had proved her extreme pacifism in the Rhineland crisis of 1936, what then was the purpose of the armaments planned by the Wehrmacht on a scale far in excess even of that of 1939? Would they have left to the Poles the provinces ceded in 1919? Or did they expect the Poles to give them up without fighting? When, in August 1938, Ewald von Kleist came to England as spokesman of the generals who were "dead against war", and Mr. Churchill said to him "that once the world was assured of a peaceful, tolerant, and law-abiding government in Germany such questions as the colonies and commercial treaties would be much easier of adjustment", Kleist replied "that his friends were not greatly concerned about the colonies, but that the Polish Corridor was the matter that affected them most" — this "was the real grievance in the military mind '.[1] And General Blaskowitz declared at Nuremberg: " I myself, as well as the whole group of German Staff and front officers, believed that . . . the question of the Polish Corridor would have to be settled some day, if necessary by force of arms ".[2]

He who creates the means can hardly disclaim the result: an army engenders force which, as " self-purpose ", is bound to unload itself sooner or later in a relentless drive for power.

For the history of the Reichswehr under the Weimar Republic Mr. Wheeler-Bennett's *Hindenburg* and the second volume of General von Rabenau's *Hans von Seekt: Aus seinem Leben*, covering the years 1918–1936, are important source books. To these is now added the brilliant short monograph by Mr. Craig on Groener's policy, 1928–1932, based on the Groener Papers recently acquired by the American National Archives; which, it is much to be hoped, he will follow up with more extensive publications. Groener, Reichswehr Minister in Brüning's Cabinet in 1930–1932, and during the last months also Minister of the Interior, made an attempt to oppose National Socialism; but when he dissolved the S.A. he was forced out of office by the Army chiefs: " The Reichswehr demonstrated its unwillingness to block Hitler's path to power ". To Groener the Army was the guardian of the national interest, of the unity of the Reich, and of national development: " the one element of stability in a world of political flux ". He demanded from it and for it a position " above parties " — *Überparteilichkeit*: a rôle similar to that which Crown and Civil Service play in this country. But he claimed for it also " the right to define the national interest " — a paramount political

[1] *Documents on British Foreign Policy, 1919–1939*, Third Series, vol. ii, pages 687-8.

[2] Nuremberg Documents, 3706-PS.

function. His was, in fact, an " idealized conception of the army ", whose leaders were neither as intelligent nor as disinterested individually as he wished to believe. " The officers' corps ", writes Mr. Craig, " was potentially the most dangerous dissident group in Germany "; " always alarmingly susceptible to the arguments of groups which claimed to be ' more National ' than the republican parties ". When in 1930 three junior officers were tried for making Nazi propaganda in the Army, their regimental commander, Beck, the later C.G.S., stood up for them — with " an independence and frankness ", says his biographer, which very nearly caused Groener to dismiss him from the service. He was dissuaded by the Commander-in-Chief, General Hammerstein, who later on strongly opposed the decree dissolving the S.A. On May 13, 1932, dissatisfaction over that decree within the ranks of the Reichswehr and intrigues in the Reichswehr Ministry encouraged by Groener's closest associate, General Schleicher, forced Groener to resign.[1] On May 22 he wrote to a friend: " Now it will be up to the generals to see that the army does not in the end kiss Herr Schicklgruber's hands like hysterical women ".

The King of Prussia and German Emperor ranked as the first soldier in the State, and was the real (or imaginary) Commander-in-Chief of its armed forces, connected with them directly, without ministerial interposition. The War Minister, although a general on the active list, dealt merely with army administration, like the British Secretary at War in the eighteenth century, when the Commander-in-Chief or the Master-General of the Ordnance represented the army in the Effective Cabinet, whenever representation was considered neces-

[1] A personal element, so far unexplained, seems to have entered into the matter, as neither Hammerstein nor Schleicher really favoured Hitler.

sary. Similarly in Prussia-Germany, the Chief of the General Staff or the Quartermaster-General was the political spokesman of the Army: the elder Moltke rather than Roon, Schlieffen and Hindenburg-Ludendorff rather than their War Ministers, whose very names are by now forgotten. The monarch was the link between the armed forces and the civilian administration, and also between Army and Navy; and it was through him that, in the last resort, the Services exerted their influence in the State. The Weimar Republic started with genuine civilians for President (Ebert) and for *Reichswehrminister* (Noske, succeeded by Gessler); the President retained the nominal supreme command, but the War Minister, in accordance with the parliamentary system, intervened between him and the armed forces; yet even so that Minister stood in a relation to the President rather different from the rest of the Cabinet, and formed a more permanent element in the administration: some twenty Governments held office under the Weimar Republic, but only four War Ministers. And such was the respect which even the Socialists had for the Army, and such was the force of its tradition, that the Reichswehr, under its own chiefs (Groener, succeeded by Seeckt), retained virtual autonomy in the State. " Seeckt ", writes Hossbach, " was the monarch of the Army "; which, morally unattached to the Republic, at best coldly tolerated its civilian rulers (during the Kapp *Putsch* Seeckt " went on leave ", deeming it inadmissible for one part of the Reichswehr to fight another). But soon personal ambitions weakened its inner coherence: in the winter of 1925–1926, a " political department " was formed in the War Ministry under Colonel von Schleicher, who, during the preceding five years, had dealt as Seeckt's assistant with the public relations and political concerns of the Reichswehr, now withdrawn from the competence of the Army Command.

In 1926, with Hindenburg for President, the Army regained its own chief in him who was nominally the first civilian in the State; and Hindenburg, impatient of genuine civilians meddling in military affairs, soon saw to it that the War Minister, too, should be a general in mufti (Groener, succeeded by Schleicher). But with political soldiers in office the power of the War Office continued to grow at the expense of the Army Command, and there was even less inclination to let political business revert to them; while with the decay of the parliamentary régime the armed forces were becoming a decisive factor on the home front. The War Office had been before 1918 an administrative office; between 1919 and 1925, the civilian façade of an autonomous Reichswehr; since 1926, its political centre; and next it started developing into what is usually called a Ministry of Defence — the advent of an air force increased the need of co-ordination between the Services. But in view of the pre-eminent importance of the Army, the chief superimposed on the three Services was a soldier, which was not to the advantage of the Army Command; for as a soldier he was apt and able to arrogate to himself more and more of its functions, and even to short-circuit it by dealing directly with subordinate commands. The office subsequently known as the *Wehrmacht-Amt* continued to grow in size and importance; and since Schleicher had created his political department, intrigue was almost a tradition within it. Officers released from close contact with their own corps and the immediate impact of its corporate opinion were more open to outside influences; and those who were out to play their own hand welcomed such release. With the death of Hindenburg the Army lost its supreme chief steeped in the old Prussian Army tradition. Hitler stepped into his place: Chancellor and Führer, civilian dictator and, first and foremost, party leader, he assumed also the supreme command of the armed forces. Henceforth the " politics " of the Army turned on its relations with Hitler and the Nazi Party. But the *Wehrmacht* Command, which should have been its defence against encroachments, became the hunting ground of Hitler's military sycophants such as Keitel (and also of exponents of new military ideas who found in Hitler an ally against the conservatives of the old General Staff.) Next, the *Reichkriegsminister* and Chief of the *Wehrmacht*, Blomberg, was made also Commander-in-Chief of the three Services : a function which he could effectively discharge only with regard to the Army — the Navy, for technical reasons, retained a much higher degree of autonomy, while the Luftwaffe belonged to Göring, second only to Hitler, as Minister of Aviation member of the Reich Cabinet, Prime Minister of Prussia, head of the Gestapo, etc. But the O.K.H. (*Ober-Kommando des Heeres*) was reduced to a subordinate position ; even the crucial problem of the part which the Commander-in-Chief of the Army would play in war, and of " the influence which he was to exercise on the total complex of preparations for war (*auf die Gesamtheit der Kriegsvorbereitung*) remained an open question ".

Hossbach, whose name is widely known through the notes he took of the conference at the Reich Chancery on November 5, 1937, is usually described as Hitler's A.D.C. In reality he retained his post on the General Staff, but was assigned to Hitler as *liaison* with the *Wehrmacht* when, in August 1934, Hitler assumed Hindenburg's place. Hossbach's title was *Adjutant der Wehrmacht beim Führer und Reichskanzler*, and assistants were joined to him representing the Navy and the Air Force ; but circumstances made him the specific spokesman of the Army, of von Fritsch, its Commander-in-Chief, and of Beck, the C.G.S. Blomberg was in constant touch with Hitler, and even more so was Göring, while Fritsch had no direct access to him, and Beck, during his five years as C.G.S., saw Hitler on business but once for five minutes. To these two men representing the Army and its Prussian-German tradition, Hossbach felt bound by ties of official loyalty and personal devotion, far more than to Hitler — " it was always our opinion ", said Göring at Nuremberg, " that Hossbach was never a warm supporter of the Führer ". He remained with Hitler till February 1938, when Hitler, by an unspeakably dirty manœuvre, rid himself of Fritsch (in which crisis Hossbach played an honourable and courageous part); and he continued on the General Staff till, at the end of August 1938, Beck resigned in protest against Hitler's Czech policy.

Hossbach's book is an apologia for the Army Command and the part it played during the years 1934–1938; he describes life in Hitler's *entourage*, and relates the story of the Blomberg-Fritsch crisis and of Beck's resignation; gives an account of the Army Command during the inter-war period, and especially between 1934 and 1938, and of its relations with Hitler and with the O.K.W.; and ponders over the rôle of the Army in German national life, and the way in which its leaders acted in the difficult and changing circumstances of the post-1918 period. His thesis in brief is this: that during the years 1934–1938, in spite of the depressed position of the Army Command, Fritsch and Beck managed to uphold the professional and moral traditions of the Prussian-German Army; that during that period the Army was on the whole immune from Hitler's encroachments — in spite of Blomberg, who, impulsive, unstable, and submissive to Hitler, intercalated himself between him and the Army, engrossing the influence due to the real army chiefs in great political decisions; that the Army was built up by Fritsch and Beck as a defensive force, and not as an instrument of aggression; and that during those years there was no reason to suppose that Hitler would use it to such purpose, or assume direct control over it. The book, factual yet highly coloured in outlook, is instructive though not always convincing: a sincere *ex parte* statement which at times tries to prove too much.

> I frankly admit [writes Hossbach] that I was one of those Germans who, in the political and economic disarray of the early thirties, set their hopes on the new Government established under the wing of Hindenburg, and not one of those who foresaw already in 1933, still less before, how matters would develop up to 1945.

In other words, he was not put off by Hitler's personality, methods, and doctrines, and failed to foresee the disaster: wherein Hossbach was representative of the Germans, and especially of German officers (including men like Beck and Canaris who were soon to become opponents of Hitler and finally his victims). They had yet to learn — and how many Germans know it even now? — that morality, more even than peace, " is indivisible ". Hossbach's picture of Hitler shows no hostile bias; or else he could hardly have stood Hitler and life in his household for three and a half years; moreover, at that time staggering successes and unmeasured adulation had not yet released all the evil in Hitler. (None the less, the account ends by being about as damning as anything written of him.) Life was chaotic and work irregular; feverish activity alternated with apathy; " Hitler and his *entourage* lived in a hothouse atmosphere ". But he did not invariably monopolize the conversation; it was as yet possible, when alone with him, to speak frankly or even to contradict him; and Hossbach denies having ever witnessed Hitler completely losing self-control, or heard of any such case from an eye-witness (possibly " carpet-biting " was a later stage of his hysteria, or is a legend). In Hitler's arrangements the *Wehrmacht* received preferential treatment; he was strictly on time on military occasions; and he showed elaborate politeness to distinguished old generals. Hossbach himself claims to have been treated with respect and regard. In short, with the *Wehrmacht* Hitler still minded his p's and q's. Whereas even before 1938 Hitler exercised a very marked influence on the pace, size, and character of the rearmament, he did not interfere with the choice and promotion of officers or with army training. During manœuvres, when things were explained to him, he would express no opinion.

> In my experience, in the years 1934–38, Hitler was completely ignorant of strategy and tactics, and I did not even think that he took any interest in them. . . .
>
> Even now I do not believe that at that time Hitler thought of assuming the command. . . .
>
> During that time Hitler strictly observed the delimitation of responsibilities between him and his military advisers . . . it will not be possible to name a case of his having arbitrarily intervened in military affairs without previous consultation with the War Minister. . . .

It was Blomberg who was to blame.

> While up to February 4, 1938, relations between Fritsch and Hitler developed with due regard for the dignity of the General, and were not harmful to the cause [of the Army], relations between Blomberg and Fritsch deteriorated steadily. . . .
>
> The years from 1934 to the beginning of 1938 are filled by a struggle of the Army Command against the *Wehrmacht* Minister and his advisers. . . .

Here, then, was an inner feud within the military camp, fit to make Hossbach take a more lenient view of Hitler's rôle and actions.

Blomberg was Hindenburg's choice, but became Hitler's man; Fritsch thinks that Reichenau (who had been Blomberg's Chief of Staff in East Prussia) may have brought him to the attention of the Party. Blomberg, in turn, made Reichenau head of the *Wehrmacht-Amt*, and next tried to place him at the head of the Army. This the Party meant to merge into the S.A., which, writes Fritsch, " would have destroyed its military and moral foundations " for years to come. In January 1934 Hindenburg forced Hitler and Blomberg to accept Fritsch as chief of the Army; June 30, 1934, broke the power of the S.A.; henceforth the conflict was between the Army and the S.S. backed by the Party. Their idea was to limit the Army to its purely technical sphere, and to take over completely the education of the Germans in the *Jung-Volk*, *Hitler-Jugend*, Labour Service, and in para-military and professional organizations. According to Hossbach, during those years Hitler repeatedly saved the Army from attacks by the Party; perhaps he did not as yet feel sufficiently certain of himself, or perhaps he meant to act as Hindenburg's heir. But Blomberg and the *Wehrmacht-Amt* are accused of having sold the pass. It was he who as representative of the armed forces agreed to Hitler stepping into Hindenburg's shoes; who made the armed forces take a personal oath of loyalty to Hitler; who, while tightening his own hold on the Army, left the Luftwaffe to Göring; and who, finally, when the generals demanded his removal because of his having contracted an unsuitable marriage, took his revenge on them first by proposing Göring for his successor, and next that Hitler himself should become *de facto* head of the *Wehrmacht*. But hardly sufficient credit is given by Hossbach to Blomberg for opposing Hitler's plans for war on November 5, 1937. Hossbach's story deserves close attention. Still, it is asking too much of the reader to believe that the Führer, while strutting in riding-boots at the head of uniformed masses, excluded military ambitions from his thoughts; that the megalomaniac who deemed his creed and " fanaticism " more effective than all professional knowledge, recognized his military incompetence; that in Hindenburg's place he meant to play Ebert; and that his assumption of the real command was a sudden inspiration or aberration engendered by having, during his visit to Rome in September 1937, seen Mussolini play that part. When Hossbach states that previous to November 5, 1937, he never noted any symptoms of Hitler planning war, the reader has merely to refer to Beck's memorandum of May 3, 1937, dealing with an order to prepare plans for a sudden operation (*schlagartig als Überfall*) against the south-east, and to that of May 20, about armed intervention in Austria in case of an attempted Habsburg restoration. Or again, Hossbach quotes the fortifications in the west, planned as the work of many years, as evidence of the "defensive intentions" of the German Army leaders. But whatever the time required to obtain perfection, no one ever doubted the purpose of those fortifications: on May 18, 1936, Neurath, then Foreign Minister, told the American diplomatist Mr. Bullitt that Germany would pursue a peaceful policy with regard to Austria and Czechoslovakia till the "fortifications are constructed and the countries of Central Europe realize that France cannot enter German territory at will".

Apparently the title of Foerster's book on Beck was to have been *A C.G.S. Fights against Hitler*;[1] now it is *A General Fights against War*. Against war as such? "Certainly Beck was no pacifist!"—but he demanded "a policy on a moral basis." Those who knew Beck testify to the nobility of his character and mind. Yet his ethos was that of the Prussian Army. He felt a growing aversion to Hitler, to his gangster mentality and methods, and to his sinister, fantastic schemes. But would Beck have dis-

[1] It is quoted under that title as a "forthcoming" book in Hossbach, *op. cit.* page 68, n. 1.

avowed the deeds of Frederick II or of Bismarck as *unsittlich*? Would he have insisted on negotiation as sole method for changing peace treaties? He protested in his writings against premature war, before rearmament had reached the level he deemed necessary — a war in which Germany might again be overwhelmed by a hostile coalition. His apprehensive calculations and forecasts, political and military, proved singularly inaccurate: he knew Germany's weakness, but he overrated the political wisdom and courage of the Western Governments, the strength of the French Army, and he treated as axiomatic hostile action by Soviet Russia. Perhaps the unconscious aversion to war of a real *Frontkämpfer* warped his judgment. But the claim that Hitler's catastrophic end has proved Beck right is hardly valid: neither the attack on Russia, nor perhaps even the defeat was inevitable, and the respective share of responsibility of Hitler and the generals for either still remains to be fixed.

When on October 1, 1933, Beck was appointed Chief of the, as yet camouflaged, General Staff, he told a friend of his fears " that we may be drawn into war before we are in a position to count on a successful defensive ". In May 1934 he gave a warning against too quick an increase of the German Army lest France should be provoked to act. After June 30, 1934 (which abroad has " evoked horror and disgust "), and the murder of Dollfuss on July 25, Beck wrote:

> Our international position is hopeless. Everything is in danger, especially our entire rearmament. All that has been laboriously achieved in that respect is lost. All Powers that matter are against us.

Again he saw a menacing France in the background.

When, in May 1937, operative preparations were ordered for a sudden attack against the south-east, Beck wrote that if the intention was to attack Czechoslovakia he would resign, not feeling " equal to the task ". And on May 20:

> My knowledge of Austria, and especially the Austrian Army, convinces me that German military intervention against a Habsburg restoration would result in war between Germany and Austria. In that case we must count with France and Czechoslovakia as enemy No. 1, with Britain, Belgium, and Russia as enemy No. 2, and with Poland and Lithuania as enemy No. 3. . . .
>
> Germany, as far as her Army is concerned, is not in a position to provoke the risk of a Central European war. And her material resources are altogether inadequate for making war, either now or in the near future.

In a memorandum of January 11, 1937, addressed to Fritsch, Beck spoke of the fear widely felt in Germany of a new war, and of the Army having to prevent a catastrophic defeat which would destroy its prestige. When reading the minutes of the Council of November 5, 1937, he was horrified by the levity of Hitler's program. Here are his reflections on " case 3 " — " if France was tied down by war with a third State ":

> France will still always have sufficient forces available against Germany. . . . It is not disputed that, if opportunity offers, it would be advisable to settle matters with Czechoslovakia (also perhaps with Austria), and that the problem should be examined and preparations made within the limits of what is feasible.

But a " far more thorough and comprehensive examination " than seems to have been given to it is required.

The trumped-up charges of homosexuality against Fritsch, and the manner in which Hitler handled them, were typical of the régime, but as for once they concerned the foremost representative of the officer class, they produced a reaction such as no outrages or atrocities committed on less privileged individuals could evoke from the presumed military guardians of German honour and *Sittlichkeit*. Indeed, " active resistance was seriously considered ", but dismissed as it would have meant civil war " without prospect of success " ; and even for a joint *démarche*, such as throwing up of commissions by the leading generals, the necessary unanimity was lacking. A joint *démarche* was again considered after a court martial, presided over by Göring, had, on March 18, acquitted Fritsch : it was proposed to demand his rehabilitation, and changes in the top ranks of the Gestapo. And again nothing happened. Beck wrote : " The Fritsch case has opened up a chasm between Hitler and the officers' corps . . . which can never be closed again ". But generals keen on making a career continued to flit across it, even when the future of the nation was at stake. " Gifts and field-marshals' batons ", wrote von Hassell in his *Diary* on April 20, 1943, " are more important to them than great historical issues and moral values."

Hitler was preparing to attack Czechoslovakia, and on May 5, 1938, Beck submitted to the new Commander-in-Chief, Brauchitsch, a warning memorandum, again singularly wrong in its premises and conclusions. Through agreement with Italy, he argued, Britain had gained freedom of action ; the war between Japan and China had eased her military position ; Britain and France had drawn closer together, politically and militarily ; " Russia must more and more be looked upon as a certain enemy of Germany " ; in a war between the Western Powers and Germany, Belgium and Holland would in time be forced to give up their neutrality towards Germany ; etc. He did not doubt that France would stand by her obligations to Czechoslovakia.

> The French Army is and remains intact, and is at present still always the strongest in Europe. . . . The position of the Government and its determination have been fortified by Daladier's recent talks in

> London. . . . It is probable that on the first day [of war] Britain will come out on the side of France. . . . Britain would hardly give us a free hand with regard to Czechoslovakia.

The one point on which Beck's opinion must be accepted — for who could know the facts better than he? — is that the *Wehrmacht* was as yet utterly unprepared for serious war. But the seriousness of any situation largely depends on the character and determination of the opponents.

A further memorandum, which was submitted by Beck to Brauchitsch on May 30, follows similar lines. But he wrote: " It is true that Czechoslovakia in the form imposed by the Versailles *Diktat*, is unbearable for Germany . . ."; which suggests a difference of tactics rather than of purpose. On July 16, Beck once more examined the situation in a long memorandum, based on his knowledge of Germany's unpreparedness, and on the assumption that the Western Powers would act (that memorandum, often referred to at Nuremberg, is now printed for the first time). " There is no chance within measurable time of smashing Czechoslovakia by military action without immediately provoking counteraction by France and England." And he concluded:

> On the basis of the above data I now feel in duty bound . . . to ask insistently that the Supreme Commander of the *Wehrmacht* [Hitler] should be made to stop the preparations he has ordered for war, and to postpone his intention of solving the Czech problem by force till the military situation is basically changed. For the present I consider it hopeless, and this view is shared by all my Quarter-masters-General and departmental chiefs of the General Staff who would have to deal with the preparation and execution of a war against Czecho-slovakia.

On the same day he proposed to Brauchitsch a joint *démarche* of the leading generals with Hitler; and that if

Hitler refused to halt his war preparations, they should all resign their commissions:

> A soldier who holds a leading position and at such a time limits his duty and task to his military charge, without being conscious of his supreme responsibility toward the nation, shows lack of greatness and of understanding of his task.

Three days later Beck went even farther in his proposal for a joint *démarche.* He foresaw that it might lead to a show-down with the Nazis, and had recourse to the traditional fiction: the Führer had to be " rescued " from the pressure of evil elements. He sketched a program in " short and clear slogans ":

> For the Führer, against war, against the *Bonzokratie*, peace with the Church, freedom of speech and Press, an end to *Cheka* methods, rule of law in the Reich, cutting of taxes by half, no more building of palaces, houses for the *Volksgenossen.* Prussian cleanliness and simplicity!

And again on July 29 he pressed Brauchitsch to tell Hitler that Germany was in no way prepared for war, and that he (Brauchitsch) and the leading generals could not accept the responsibility for it. " The wording of that declaration could not be too emphatic, hard, and brutal." About the beginning of August Beck drafted an address which he wanted Brauchitsch to deliver to a gathering of the commanding generals. It follows the lines of Beck's previous memoranda, envisages even wider horizons, but again overrates the moral and mental level both of the German generals and of the men then in office in Paris and London: the one who would have led England in the sense foreshadowed by Beck was as yet excluded from all share in government.

> I am convinced [Beck wanted Brauchitsch to say] that England, should Germany insist on solving the

> Czech problem by force, will enter the war at the side of France. . . . Once she resolves to do so, it is war to the end. For England will fight not so much with a view to preserving Czechoslovakia, which will be a side issue, as to knocking out the new Germany, in which she sees the aggressor and a danger to the basic elements of British political ideology: justice, Christianity, and toleration.

He wanted Brauchitsch to conclude with the following appeal to the generals:

> I must therefore demand from you gentlemen, that you should, come what may, support me and unconditionally follow me along the path which I must tread for the weal of our German Fatherland.

It was perhaps naïve of Beck to think that a man could be made to deliver such an address: sense, courage, and character cannot be transmitted from him who has them to him who has not. At the beginning of August Brauchitsch summoned a conference of commanding generals; Beck read to them his memorandum of July 16; General Adam, commander designate on the western front, described as utterly insufficient the western fortifications and the forces available for that front (five active and four reserve divisions, and some *Landwehr*). Everyone, except Reichenau and Busch, agreed in opposing war. Brauchitsch stated that there was such agreement, but made no appeal to the generals.

> Beck resigned, indignant and unbending [writes Hassell]. . . . Brauchitsch hitched his collar a notch higher and said: " I am a soldier; it is my duty to obey ".

No one followed Beck. Halder accepted his succession. When Ewald von Kleist, risking his life,[1] came to London with the report that all the generals were against war but

[1] He was executed after July 20, 1944.

required encouragement from the West, Neville Chamberlain wrote to Halifax on August 19:[1]

> I take it that von Kleist is violently anti-Hitler, and is extremely anxious to stir up his friends in Germany to make an attempt at its [*sic*] overthrow. He reminds me of the Jacobites at the Court of France in King William's time and I think we must discount a good deal of what he says.

Chamberlain, for one, had made up his mind whom to trust and with whom to play.

[1] *B.D.* Third Series, vol. ii, page 686.

HALDER ON HITLER

HAD Hitler been killed or overthrown on July 20, 1944, a substantial tribute of Allied gratitude would have been expected by the Germans for having knocked out their Führer when he was anyhow reeling to his doom. Anything short of their expectations — of a bill of indemnity for the past and immunity from penalties, of the post-Munich frontiers with Danzig and the Corridor thrown in — would have been decried as " a vile betrayal ". On the other hand, Hitler's removal before he had run his course would have enabled Nazi propagandists to assert that but for the " stab in the back " Germany would never have lost the war: the position would have been retrieved by Hitler's genius, as it was by Frederick's in the Seven Years' War. But Hitler escaped death and the generals flinched — German merit, Allied treachery, and the story about the filched victory were buried in a common grave. None the less a new German " stab in the back " story could be expected to emerge — but from which quarter and in what form? Indeed, two such stories have by now been given currency by the same man, General Franz Halder, Chief of the General Staff from September 1938 till September 1942. The victim (twice stabbed) is the German Army Command, first by Neville Chamberlain, and next by Hitler: had not Chamberlain gone to Munich, the German generals would have removed Hitler; and had it not been for Hitler's meddling incompetence, they would, in their own good time, have reversed the verdict of 1918, or they might even have won the war prematurely brought on by him in 1939.

In the testimony taken at Nuremberg on February 25-26, 1946, Halder gave his account of the army plot of 1938. He claims to have discussed "the forcible removal of Hitler" with General Beck, his predecessor as C.G.S., with Admiral Canaris and General Oster of the Military Intelligence, and with Field-Marshal von Witzleben, in 1938 Commander of the Berlin Military District (by 1946 all four were dead). According to Halder, during the first days of September 1938, Witzleben came to discuss with him the overthrow of Hitler. Witzleben drew up the plan. Halder himself did not talk about it to anyone else; for anyone who knew of it was a danger. It was for Witzleben to communicate with the generals under his command. "My task was to fix the date when it should take place; and when von Witzleben had done his part, to initiate the Commander-in-Chief of the Army, Brauchitsch". Had not Chamberlain come to Munich, the plan would have been executed — such is Halder's story; but seeing how hesitant he himself was ever after, how many excuses for inaction were found by disaffected generals both before and after Munich, and how they faltered on July 20, 1944, can one assume that things would have been different in September 1938?

Of Hitler's military advisers, Blomberg, Fritsch, Beck, Brauchitsch, Keitel and Jodl are dead, and Halder is now probably the man best qualified to speak from personal experience about Hitler as military leader: an account by him written with impartiality and detachment would be of the highest historical value. The present pamphlet [1] is not: in spite of a rich factual background, it fails to carry conviction on some of the crucial issues; argumentative, often querulous, and poorly constructed, it is an indictment by one who served Hitler — cowed, exasperated, and insulted, obeying even against his better professional judgment until dismissed. Now Halder tries to

[1] Franz Halder, *Hitler als Feldherr*. Münchener Dom-Verlag.

enlighten the German public on the military qualifications, abilities, and achievements of the man who in his glory was acclaimed as *der grösste Feldherr aller Zeiten* (" the greatest military leader of all time "), but in his decline was referred to, in deriding abbreviation, as *der Gröfaz*. How far the pamphlet will achieve its purpose will depend on the mood of the masses, who accept or reject an account or argument not for its cogency but according to their own bent of the moment.

Hitler, according to Halder, lacked the necessary qualities and knowledge effectively to direct large-scale modern military operations. (" It needs no proving ", said the chimney-sweep to the chambermaid when she informed him that he was not a gentleman.) He had not the long sight, the methodical approach, the patience, the clear, steady purpose, and the secure touch of the experienced commander. Instead, he relied on the " intuitions " of his untrained mind and undisciplined nature, and claimed for them infallibility. Even when good strategic ideas occurred to him, he was incapable of thinking them out to the end. He had undoubtedly been the driving force behind Germany's rapid rearmament; but, obsessed by numbers, he sacrificed quality to quantity, and destroyed more than he could create; " inner fissures ", of which Hitler would take no account, soon appeared in the hastily constructed military edifice. Similarly in the Luftwaffe his " intoxication with figures and political impatience defeated the military need of sound organic growth ". And then, of his own choice and without pressure of external circumstances, he recklessly risked war. " An irresponsible gambler with human lives ", in the pursuit of his fantastic schemes Hitler chose to ignore the limits of what was feasible. He profoundly distrusted the Army Command — the professional soldiers and their traditions — and was jealous of them. A new explanation is given by Halder of Hitler's withdrawal of the German armoured divisions before Dunkirk: Göring had warned him not to leave the victory and its glory to the generals, and undertaken to annihilate, by means of the Luftwaffe alone, the enemy who was by now almost completely encircled. Personal ambitions and party interests came first, and Nazi fanaticism was expected to work miracles. Therefore Hitler loathed having to hand over his young Nazis to Army leaders whom he considered soulless and fossilized: he went in for separate formations withdrawn from under their command; but, according to Halder, he had no true feeling for his soldiers, nor any deeper connexion with them. In his overweening conceit, he would not merely determine the strategy of the war, but even interfere with its actual conduct, issuing at times insane orders, as that which, when the war in Russia took an unfavourable turn, forbade all withdrawal. "The man, for whom the masterpiece of a modern General Staff map was an insoluble puzzle, would during the Russian campaign take it upon himself to interfere from his Headquarters, hundreds of miles behind the front, with the dispositions of individual divisions, or to decide on tactical detail, solely within the competence of the commander on the spot." Many examples of Hitler's disastrous interventions are quoted: an indictment which could have been formidable.

Yet much of it is irrelevant. There was little difference between Hitler and his generals in their ultimate aims: the issue between them was technical rather than moral. Both sides were out to rebuild Germany's armed forces, to re-establish her military preponderance, and then, by intimidation or by war, to realize her territorial ambitions — the Army, secretly and illegally built up in pre-Hitler days, was not for defence only. But anyone who prepares war gambles with human lives, and gamblers are not judged by the degree of orthodoxy with which they play their game. On the level on which Halder builds up his case against Hitler, success is the test; and Hitler was amazingly successful till he launched his attack against Russia, which, of all his undertakings, receives the greatest measure of approval and justification from Halder.

"Whoever did not know Adolf Hitler", declared Halder at Nuremberg, "cannot imagine what a master of deception and camouflage the man was"; and he claims to have told General Beck "that with such a man or beast you can only compete by using force". This the Western statesmen did not, or would not, see, and they let themselves be bluffed by him. Here Halder's case begins to break down. Did Hitler take excessive risks in 1936 and 1938? When moral considerations are discarded, all that matters is that he pulled it off: he traversed the danger zone of rearmament, undoubtedly helped by his bluff with figures; and by his bloodless conquests of Austria and Czechoslovakia, connived in or even aided by the appeasers, he completely transformed the strategic position and the balance of power in Europe. In 1939 he again tried to pull it off without war, but on May 23 he told the generals: "We cannot expect a repetition of the Czech affair". And on August 22:

> The creation of a Greater Germany was a great political achievement, but open to question on the military side, since it was achieved through the bluff of the political leaders. It has now to be tested in war: if possible . . . by solving the tasks one by one.

Did he, then, go to war with an army whose shortcomings and "fissures" he chose to ignore? But does this matter when the army proved equal to the task? Halder, the German technician, seems to resent even victories won against the professional rules of the game. There is something comic about the following passage. After the conquest of Poland, according to Halder:

> Hitler was faced with a typical strategic problem to be decided on the basis of military and of weighty political considerations. The answer given by the General Staff was characteristic of the German soldiers. When powerful German forces were released from Poland, they favoured a defensive deployment in the West. After Germany's victory in Poland, a frontal attack by the Western Powers against the Siegfried Line and the Upper Rhine had lost all chance of success. To attain a decision by arms, to which the Western Powers themselves had appealed, they would have had to attack the unfortified German frontiers across neutral territory. Then the possibility would have arisen by a strategic counter-move decisively to defeat the attacking enemy forces, away from their French base and from the saving coast.
>
> Such a solution, which leaves the initiative to the enemy, is only possible for a commander equally certain of his troops and of his own skill. It did not appeal to the dictator, altogether shaky in questions of military leadership. The bitter controversy was settled by a peremptory order from Hitler. . . .

Thus it was Hitler who, against protests from the General Staff, cut short the " phoney war ". The writings of the Chiefs of the two General Staffs, Halder and Gamelin, make one feel that the supreme decisions about military matters had best be left to intelligent civilians advised by comparatively junior, unorthodox soldiers. In 1940 Orde Wingate, talking to me, ascribed a certain bold and successful decision to Hitler ; when I asked how he knew, he replied : " Because the generals would have been too timid ".

That Halder should even now assert the superiority of a defensive strategy in the West, which would have left France undefeated and Britain with a base on the Continent, seems the more surprising in view of his estimate of the position in the East in 1941. He records that the

Army Command earnestly warned Hitler against attacking Russia, and that it proved very hard for Hitler to take that decision. But next he upholds Hitler's view " that Russia was preparing to attack Germany ", and asserts that " we now know on good authority " that Hitler was right.

> Russia [writes Halder] would naturally have timed the attack so as to catch Germany at the most unfavourable moment, that is, when the West could once more become active. Thus the war on two fronts was imminent, which the memorandum of the General Staff had foretold in 1938.
>
> If the politician sees no further possibility of settling a dangerous conflict by diplomatic means, the military commander cannot be blamed for wishing to protect his own country against the enemy by means of an attack, provided the politician gives him a chance to do so in accordance with international law and conventions. . . .
>
> The general must, however, make clear to the politician what is militarily possible, and this must determine the war aims of the politician.
>
> Early in 1941 the German forces . . . available for the Eastern front would have sufficed to defeat decisively Russia's European armies, and thereby to paralyse for a considerable time all Russian military action. They would further have sufficed to provide, by occupying large parts of the Ukraine, White Russia, and the Baltic States, a strategic cover for the German and Rumanian frontiers, and a gage for peace negotiations.

If this was the opinion given to Hitler by the General Staff simultaneously with warnings against attacking Russia, it is hard to see what purpose such warnings were to serve, except of an alibi in case of failure.

Halder even now feels uncertain as to when Hitler finally decided to attack Russia; and he puts forward two incompatible views, apparently without noticing the contradiction. Thus on page 36:

> It can be assumed that the final decision was taken only after the quick successes of the Balkan campaign, which disclosed beyond all doubt Russia's hostile attitude to Hitler.

But on page 39:

> With the opening of operations against Russia delayed for about eight weeks by the unforeseen intermezzo of the Yugoslav campaign and the unavoidable extension of that against Greece, Hitler obviously stood under pressure of the advanced season.

And Halder adds:

> What in previous campaigns was rare, now was of daily occurrence. Hitler took a hand in the detailed exercise of operative command.

It would be presumptuous in anyone, except a foremost expert in possession of the fullest material, to controvert technical judgments of the German C.G.S. about the campaign. But even the ordinary reader cannot help being struck by certain admissions and omissions. Concerning the immediate objectives, there was, says Halder, no fundamental difference of opinion: these were the Lower Dnieper in the south, the high ground east of Smolensk in the centre, and the region of Leningrad in the north. But the next sentence suggests that Hitler was not the only one whose thoughts already wandered beyond the limits of what was previously considered feasible for the German forces.

> The further objectives would depend on the outcome of the first big battles. But one thing was clear: Moscow, as the centre of the Russian system of communications and as one of the chief arsenals of European Russia, round which a considerable part of her new formations was bound to gather, retained surpassing importance.

> A remark to the effect by the C.-in-C. [Brauchitsch] produced a curiously excited and sharp rejoinder from Hitler. . . . Only a completely calcified brain, enmeshed in the conceptions of past centuries, he said, could attach such importance to the capital of the country. His own interest turned to the hatching grounds of Bolshevism — Leningrad and Stalingrad. If these were destroyed by far-flung movements of strong army-groups in the North and South, Bolshevism would be dead, and that was what mattered.

And farther on Halder speaks of the " mystic fixation " of Hitler on Leningrad and Stalingrad, " talismans of Bolshevism ", whose loss, he thought, would deprive Bolshevism of " its last strength ". Fetishism of names is consonant with Hitler's primitive, superstitious mentality. But was not Stalingrad of supreme strategic importance? Its capture would have cut both the land and river transport of Caucasian oil, indispensable to Russia's armed forces and to her agriculture. This is never mentioned by Halder — it is common among German controversialists to damage their case by such omissions and exaggerations. For the case against Hitler over the Russian campaign is strong, and both the blunders and the fury of the raving megalomaniac grew with the reverses. The arguments between him and the General Staff (presumably Halder himself) " reached boiling point ". Told about the appearance of fresh Russian divisions, he taxed the General Staff " in the bitterest words with lacking *élan*, even with cowardice masquerading as sober realism ", and declared that only those naïve simpletons the theoreticians " could be taken in by Stalin's clumsy swindle ". And when shown a list of Stalin's probable resources in men and tanks, Hitler, " foaming at the mouth and with clenched fists went for the reporting officer and said he would not put up with such idiotic chatter ". Finally Halder was dismissed.

> The short personal talk at the end of a service report was characteristic. Hitler bitterly complained of constant and sharp dissent, and enumerated, quoting exact dates, the many occasions on which dissent had led to dramatic scenes that deeply hurt him. This constant struggle consumed half his nervous strength. Its cost was excessive. The tasks which now faced the army required " not professional skill, but the fervour of the National-Socialist faith ", which he could not expect from an officer of the old school. He further remarked that " also the secret of Moltke's successes was in the fervour of his monarchical convictions ".

Reading the grim story of the Russian campaign, one is less surprised at the renewed conspiratorial talk among the highest generals, reported *e.g.* by Hassel, than at their inaction. Was September 29, 1938, the only possible date?

Halder has now come forward as witness, and in his pamphlet has volunteered evidence about the Russian campaign and his personal relations with Hitler. It would be interesting to learn more about both. He is known to have kept a diary. He said at Nuremberg: ". . . all my shorthand diaries have been taken away by the Gestapo ". And here is a statement by Major-General Telford Taylor, Chief U.S. Prosecution Counsel at the U.S. Military Tribunal Trials at Nuremberg:[1]

> The entire Jodl and Halder diaries were offered in evidence in the " High Command Case ". They are, it is believed, of such prime historical importance that they should be published in full.

It seems in the public interest that this should be done.

[1] See *International Conciliation*, April 1949, page 351.

HERBERT VON DIRKSEN

SIR NEVILE HENDERSON'S " scruples " about writing his book on the origins of the war, *The Failure of a Mission*, were " finally overcome " by the remark of the station-master of Grantham that " he and people like him know nothing of the facts of the case ", but want to know. And similarly his opposite number, Herr Herbert von Dirksen, German Ambassador in London 1938–1939, relates in the foreword to his new book, *Moskau, Tokio, London*, what it was that finally determined him. A schoolboy, who had assisted at his de-Nazification trial, " declared categorically " that in his own and his school-fellows' opinion it was now incumbent on Dirksen to write his memoirs for their instruction and enlightenment. Presumably not much persuasion was required in either case, for there was obvious readiness to speak about one-self: Henderson continued it in his self-revealing book *Water under the Bridges*, while Dirksen had started writing his autobiography about 1932, when he reached the age of 50, the modern *mezzo del cammin.* He completed the book in 1935 on his way to Japan, and had it printed for " private circulation " under the title *Zwischenbilanz* (" Interim Statement ").

From Japan he wrote to his friends in Germany circular letters, *Briefe aus Japan*, again " privately printed ". He complains in *Zwischenbilanz*: " It is the peculiar pro-fessional tragedy of the diplomatist that the most serious part of his labours, his written reports, is accessible only to a narrow circle of over-worked officials in the Foreign Office . . .". This grievance, so far as Henderson and Dirksen are concerned, is being effectively removed by the publication of the British and German diplomatic documents. Moreover, the Soviet Foreign Office has published a small volume of *Dirksen Papers*, seized at his country house in Silesia. Most interesting among them is his " Memorandum on the Development of Political Relations between Germany and Britain during my Mission in London, May 1938–August 1939 "; this, too, is something of an " interim statement ", written by a Dirksen visibly hurt by insufficient appreciation shown to him by Hitler and Ribbentrop, yet at a time when the Third Reich could still be expected to endure. Although the memorandum was clearly not for official use, there is nothing in it incompatible with the principles and spirit of the Nazi régime, and a good deal which faithfully conforms to it. Thus material is to hand for a comparative examination of Dirksen's new book; and still more will become available when the German documents covering the period from Munich to the outbreak of war are published.

Zwischenbilanz is a self-revealing but unpleasant book: mainly family history and reminiscences of childhood and youth by a highly egocentric, ambitious, bitter, and yet pliant man, who adjusted himself to situations in a cold, resentful manner. In *Zwischenbilanz* his resentments turn largely against his own parents, and his scrutiny and criticism of their failings and foibles are, to say the least, unattractive — things people discuss under psycho-analysis rather than in print. The family of Dirksen's father had for generations been Prussian Civil Servants, that of his mother Cologne bankers; but as she was intent on social advancement, they worked their way by patient " social trench-warfare " into the inner circle of the Berlin aristocracy. Dirksen gives a cruel account of those social strivings; claims to have suffered severely from them, and repeatedly reverts to the subject; asserts that to his parents even the children were mere figures on their social chess-board ; but in one passage shows redeeming insight :

> Still, I clearly recognize that it is very much easier for the son, in possession of the social position obtained by his parents, to assume a severe, Cato-like attitude ; and that as a social outsider he would perhaps have proceeded exactly like his parents.

Other, sometimes astonishing, grievances are displayed, joined to this revealing statement : " We had the reputation of being the best behaved children in Berlin, which even then I felt to be questionable praise ". Also in *Moskau, Tokio, London* he mentions the inclination to being a " model boy " (*eine sicherlich vorhandene Anlage zum Musterknaben*) : which would be of little interest if it did not reappear in the grown-up man, conforming to people whom he neither loved nor respected ; and if that *Musterknabe* — suppressing his resentments and remembering his grievances, inflated or even imaginary — was not in his bitter, revengeful egocentricism so representative of the docile and ruthless German nation.

Thinking back to the years before the First World War, Dirksen wrote in *Zwischenbilanz* :

> The danger of encirclement threatening Germany had become perfectly clear to me. The Morocco conflict, with the *Panther* leap to Agadir, had evoked in me the deepest patriotic indignation ; I felt furious that peace-loving Germany should have to suffer being reproached with disturbing the peace by an Entente thirsting for conquests. . . . I wrote an article burning with indignation, but then myself did not think it fit for print.

" With horror I became aware that Germany was not attuned, even spiritually or theoretically, to a policy of Imperialism " ; he therefore set about to elaborate its " theoretical foundations ". He writes in *Moskau, Tokio, London* : " A State gradually losing its foliage and hollowed out — that was Germany since the accession of William II ". Himself typical of the *Wilhelminische Aera*, Dirksen is hard on his makers, and, an admirer of Bismarck, reproduces him at his worst.

Born in 1882, Dirksen started his official career in the Home Service; but during the First World War he served at the front, in the German Administration in Belgium, and at the Hague Legation; and he entered the regular diplomatic service in May 1918. The next fifteen years he spent either in the East European Department of the German Foreign Office (of which department he was the head in 1925–1928), or with various diplomatic missions in Eastern Europe: he was at Kiev, 1918–1919; Chargé d'Affaires in Warsaw, 1920–1921; Consul-General at Danzig, 1923–1925; and Ambassador in Moscow, 1928–1933. The chapters on Eastern Europe, which fill about half the book, are objectively the most interesting: although much in them covers familiar ground, they add to the history of German-Polish and German-Russian relations, for which, during those years, the documentation is as yet scant.

It was an axiom with most Germans that the work of Versailles had to be undone, and that the Corridor, Upper Silesia, and the greater part of Posnania should be restored to the Reich. " It was hoped ", writes Dirksen, " to convince the world of the justice of these demands ". But apparently even in 1922 an understanding with Russia, irrespective of her régime, seemed the most telling argument: Herr von Maltzan, head of the Eastern Department, was the maker of the Rapallo Treaty, Count Brockdorff-Rantzau, Ambassador in Moscow, was, according to Dirksen, its most uncompromising exponent, and the Reichswehr under von Seeckt its firmest support.

> I myself [writes Dirksen] was in full agreement with the policy of that treaty, and I welcomed it as a mark of incipient self-confidence in our foreign policy,

and as an effective demonstration with regard to Poland.

Even Westerners among the Germans considered it " incumbent on German foreign policy " to find a counterweight to the West in good relations with Russia.

> The general attitude of the average German toward Russia can be expressed in one sentence: when our relations with Russia were good, it was good for both countries; when we were enemies, we both suffered equally.

For several years, Brockdorff-Rantzau, a real Junker, dominated Germany's East European policy. " He often reminded me of a lonely rock," writes Dirksen, " the survivor of aeons in a completely transformed world." As a conscious aristocrat he would meet men of every class and race on easy terms, " but in his inner heart only those counted who could prove 16 or 32 ancestors ". Dirksen remembers the man with the visible awe of an uncertain newcomer possessed of social ambitions and no quarterings; and his account of Brockdorff-Rantzau, to whose wilful ways others had to defer, seems suffused with the glow of " aristocracy ". " Never in his six years at Moscow did he set foot in the office-building (*Bürogebäude*) of the Embassy." In relations with Berlin,

> without ever bringing matters to a point, he let it be clearly understood that he acknowledged no superior other than the President of the Reich; and that it was a personal favour on his part if he communicated carbons of his reports to the Foreign Office.

He would announce when he was coming, but " the most intricate plans and ruses had to be devised to make him leave Berlin, as no one had the courage to tell him frankly that his official duties required his presence in

Moscow". (Dirksen was head of the East European Department during Rantzau's last three years in Russia.)

> Decisive for his career, and indeed for his life, was the "Peace" Treaty of Versailles, in whose early negotiations he had taken part as Foreign Minister. As a passionate and proud German patriot he could never forget or forgive the humiliations inflicted on him, a representative of his country and a nobleman. . . . He lived and worked for the sole purpose of obliterating the humiliation of Versailles. The Treaty of Rapallo seemed to him to serve the purpose, and he therefore readily accepted the Moscow Embassy. . . . He created the "mythos" of Rapallo, expressed in the slogans of "the spirit of Rapallo" and of "the community of fate (*Schicksalsgemeinschaft*) of the two great nations vanquished in the war".

Rantzau was therefore utterly opposed to Locarno, and shared and encouraged the suspicions and fears which it aroused in the U.S.S.R. The formula devised to prevent Germany from being obliged, under Article 16 of the League Covenant, to permit the transit of foreign troops against Russia, did not satisfy him, and he was wholly unco-operative in the negotiations for a new Russian-German Treaty complementary to Locarno: to avoid appending his name to it he would not have it signed in Moscow, and it thus became the "Berlin Treaty of 1926". In August 1928, he came home on leave, a very sick man.

> Feeling that he was dying, he dictated a farewell letter to Chicherin and Litvinov, once more testifying to his faith in German-Russian friendship, and exhorting them to continue the tradition of the Rapallo policy. In full consciousness that his end was approaching, a few hours before he died he corrected with his own hand the draft of the letter. Shortly afterwards I was called to his death-bed, and saw his finely shaped aristocratic features, still more

spiritualized (*vergeistigt*) and haughty in death than they had been in life.

Dirksen's romanticized account of Rantzau portrays its author's attitude rather than his subject: from documents found among von Seeckt's papers it is known that Rantzau was at first critical of the Rapallo Treaty, and that a memorandum of his on the *Ostpolitik*, dated July 15, 1922, provoked a few weeks later, a sharp rejoinder from Seeckt, containing the sentence: " One who thinks the Rapallo Treaty foremost a political blunder . . . seems unfit to represent Germany in Moscow ".[1] How and when Rantzau's attitude changed has still to be ascertained.

Dirksen succeeded Rantzau as Ambassador to the U.S.S.R., arriving in Moscow (if any date of his can be accepted unchecked) on January 6, 1929. In spite of the many difficulties which he had to encounter, he remained a decided adherent of German-Russian co-operation. Soon he learnt that in December 1928 the Soviet Government, without informing the Germans, had proposed non-aggression pacts to Russia's western neighbours—Litvinov's somewhat belated reply to Locarno; and before he left, the Russian-Polish non-aggression pact was signed on July 25, 1932: " but our most important demand was fully met—that there should be no trace of a Soviet guarantee for the existing German-Polish frontier ". During Dirksen's five years in Moscow there was open economic, and secret military, co-operation between the two countries. Dirksen was convinced that the Soviet Union " would develop into a sound undertaking ", and was fascinated by the " magnificently conceived plans and the ruthless determination " of the Soviet leaders in carrying them out, even at the " sacrifice of the welfare, nay the lives, of millions ". He " felt well in Moscow ";

[1] See " Der Seeckt-Plan ", in *Der Monat*, November 1948.

though incidentally he mentions that sometimes friends disappeared and "their wives committed suicide", and "news seeped through of tortures" in prisons.

Dirksen's arrival in Moscow coincided with the launching of the first Five-Year Plan: thousands of German experts and technicians were hired to help in it — "at least 5000 of them worked in the widely scattered industrial undertakings of the enormous Soviet Empire". They proved "a valuable source of information" for Dirksen. "I do not believe that any other country, either before or later, possessed such a mass of detailed information about the Soviet Union as did Germany during those years." He worked hard to interest the leading firms of the German *Schwerindustrie* in Russia, and to carry through with the help of the German Government the operations necessary to finance their contracts; he rightly regarded "credits invested in the U.S.S.R. as a productive insurance against unemployment"; during the years of the worst economic depression work was thus provided for many tens of thousands of Germans without in the end Germany suffering the least financial loss. That the industries which those German technicians helped to establish would eventually serve to defeat a German invasion Dirksen naturally could not have foreseen; and if Germany had adhered to the foreign policy of his choice, that situation would never have arisen.

> I learnt to appreciate the military co-operation of the two Army-Commands as a further important factor safeguarding the political structure. So long as there was mutual confidence in that important sphere, it was easier to overcome the effect of political storms caused by the meddling activities of the Comintern.

His own personal relations with Voroshilov "belonged to the most pleasant" he had in Moscow; but he speaks with special warmth about the Chief of the General Staff,

Marshal Yegorov, " a determined adherent of German-Russian friendship " (executed in the purge of 1936–1937). With Litvinov, too, he claims to have entertained friendly personal relations, though Litvinov was not " a convinced adherent of the Rapallo policy ", and much rather " sympathized with Great Britain ". On the other hand, Litvinov's deputy, Krestinski, who had " for many years been Soviet Ambassador in Berlin . . . felt real sympathy for Germany " (he, too, was liquidated in the purge).

Towards the end of 1932, Yegorov

> insistently urged our Military Attaché, General Köstring [a German brought up in Russia] to impress on his Government the need of deciding for the East or the West. Failing a decision, or if it favoured the West, a basic change in Soviet policy could not be avoided. . . . In this highly complex situation exploded the long-expected and apprehended bomb. . . . The National Socialists attained power.

What were going to be Hitler's policy and reactions ? The Soviet Union, which had hitherto regularly met its financial obligations, for the first time asked for a postponement of payments falling due in March and April 1933 : which, to everybody's surprise, Hitler conceded. When Dirksen came to report to him, Hitler listened,

> asked a few questions, and repeated his desire to maintain friendly relations with the Soviet Union, provided they refrained from interfering in internal German affairs. But then a scene occurred which [writes Dirksen] I have never forgotten. Hitler got up, went to the window, looked at the park of the Reich Chancellery, and remarked dreamily : " If only we could reach an understanding with Poland ! But Pilsudski is the one man with whom this could be attained ! " I replied that this would be possible only if Germany renounced her claims to the Cor-

> ridor ; and that demand, upheld by the whole of Germany, had united the Germans during the years of inner discord. Hitler dropped the subject.

The " Berlin Treaty " of 1926, concluded for five years, had come up for renewal in 1931 ; but for two years the pre-Hitler German Governments hesitated. Hitler did not, and ratifications were exchanged on May 5, 1933.

> The adherents of a German-Russian understanding were visibly delighted, while Litinov was unable to suppress his morose incredulity ; he had, it seemed, definitely turned his back on the Rapallo policy. Although things calmed down gradually . . . the situation was far from normal. An edifice, which it had taken many years of infinite effort to raise, was now being systematically demolished by both sides.

In Germany measures were taken against " Derop ", a Soviet organization for the distribution of Russian oil (and incidentally of Communist propaganda). The Russians proceeded to clear out the German engineers and technicians, of whom there was no longer the same need (and who had been supplying " a mass of detailed information " to the Embassy). Lastly, the German military authorities were informed

> that the Red Army desired to dissolve its connexions with the Reichswehr. A German delegation, headed by General von Bockelberg, arrived in Moscow, and everything was settled in a friendly spirit. The military representatives of the two countries took sorrowful leave of each other, more like friends who part not of their free will but under pressure of untoward circumstances.

Then Dirksen made a last attempt to patch up matters : Krestinski and Yenukidse, a Georgian close to Stalin, were going to Germany for the summer ; Dirksen and his Counsellor, von Twardowski, met them privately in a suburban villa:

> I discussed with them the situation, and tried to convince them that agreement was possible also with the new régime in Germany. I urged that a prominent Soviet representative should meet Hitler. Yenukidse and Krestinski seemed agreed in principle. The upshot was that Krestinski, after his cure at Kissingen, should spend a few days in Berlin and ask to be received by Hitler.

If the results of the talk were favourable, Dirksen hoped to see the bases fixed for a new economic and political understanding. While on leave in Germany he learnt from Twardowski that " Hitler was willing to receive Krestinski "; but he also learnt that he himself was being transferred to Tokyo. " I never succeeded in ascertaining the true reasons of the transfer ", writes Dirksen, adding in the same breath: " After careful consideration I reached the conclusion that it was purely a matter of routine "; and he denies having felt aggrieved at going to an Embassy with a much smaller staff than Moscow.

> In October I returned to Berlin to prepare for the closing act of my Moscow Embassy, Krestinski's visit to Hitler. But the scheme was upset. Twardowski wired he had been informed by Litvinov that Krestinski would return to Moscow by way of Vienna. I was annoyed and disappointed. . . . Subsequently I ascertained that Krestinski's visit to Berlin was cancelled on the initiative of Litvinov, who had spun a small intrigue against his colleague. He jealously watched that other officials of the Foreign Ministry should not share the limelight with him, and he may have felt hostile to what must have appeared to him as an attempt to cut across his policy of an out-and-out Western orientation.

" The greatest attraction of my new post ", writes Dirksen, " was its distance from Berlin, with the prospect of a long journey to a beautiful and interesting country." Moreover, he would be able to indulge his " passion for East Asiatic art " (and perhaps also enjoy the exchange of ceremonial compliments with Orientals). When on December 23, 1933, a Crown Prince was born in Tokyo, Dirksen (according to the American Ambassador, Mr. Grew [1]) in a message of congratulation to *Nichi Nichi*, was quoted as saying: " So soon upon my arrival at my post, I consider it a personal honour to me ". He now relished the " community of fate " between Germany and Japan, apparently unconcerned at its reactions on German-Russian relations — or did he think that everything could be settled at the expense of the Anglo-Saxon Powers? By the time he was leaving Tokyo for London he professes to have pondered on Joseph Chamberlain's plan of an alliance between Great Britain, Germany, and Japan, but does not explain how it would have squared with Germany's and Japan's overgrown ambitions — the muddled thinking of a light-weight in diplomacy, typical of post-Bismarckian Germany.

In both Germany and Japan " the age of liberalism had reached its term, and had been replaced by a totalitarian régime ". Both countries were " on the march "; " had been bound by similar fetters, had achieved ' freedom ' by similar means, and were pursuing similar aims ". Both had proved unable to fit themselves into the comity of nations, had become accustomed to unpopularity, had left the League, and were equally averse to international action. " As ' have-nots ' they aroused the hostility of the ' haves ' among the nations." And both, by different paths, had reached the same result: complete subordination of the individual to the State. They shared the " Spartan outlook ". Yet the German Army and Foreign Office favoured China; only the Nazi Party preferred Japan, carrying on negotiations

[1] J. C. Grew, *Ten Years in Japan* (1944), page 103.

through the " Bureau Ribbentrop ", behind the back of the German Foreign Office ; Dirksen heard of it from the Japanese.

He went home on leave in 1935, starting from Yokohama on the *Empress of Canada* on April 9 (page 168), and landing at Bremerhaven from the *Europa*, also on April 9 (page 182). " Compared with the miserable conditions of 1932, Germany seemed to me a changed country." Certain aspects of the régime were criticized, but Hitler's surprising actions and successes in foreign policy " filled the public with satisfaction. . . . I myself was impressed by the results achieved in so short a time." Asked to join the Nazi Party, Dirksen did so — " as I did not wish to evade declaring my allegiance to the régime I served " (a far more dignified explanation than is mostly given by German diplomatists now writing their memoirs). He found the Foreign Office completely in the dark concerning Ribbentrop's negotiations with the Japanese ; saw Ribbentrop ; but learnt most about them from the Japanese Ambassador ; and much approved of the point of the treaty being turned against the Comintern, " whose connexion with the Soviet Government was tenaciously denied by the Kremlin ". He was received by Hitler.

> I had great expectations . . . assuming that an opportunity would be given to me to report at length on the political situation in the Far East. But after two or three minutes he became restless, shifted about in his chair, and then suddenly apologized for having to break off the conversation as he had to attend to other important duties. . . . I left agape and furious.

Later on he obtained an hour's interview with Hitler, and assured him that Japan was " a reliable partner for the anti-Comintern ".

Dirksen attended that summer at the Olympic Games

held in Berlin and at the Party Rally at Nuremberg; and in his *Briefe aus Japan* describes his experiences, in good Nazi jargon, as *einmalig*.

> These masses at Nuremberg were not a mere herd of sheep, driven by orders from their masters, nor mere squads of party-men in uniform. They were unconsciously moved by the deep faith of an entire nation, ready to make sacrifices for the sake of a better future.

To those who suffered persecutions and torture he seems to have given as little thought as he gave them in Russia.

In November 1936 Dirksen returned to Japan for another two years, whose story can be studied much better in the first volume of the *Documents on German Foreign Policy*. Because of asthma, rendered worse by the Japanese climate, he asked to be released from his post, and left Japan on Sunday, February 6, 1938. The previous day the news appeared in the Press that he, Papen, and Hassell had been placed on the retired list; but on the morning of the 6th, he received a personal telegram from Neurath denying that report — and wondered how such erroneous news could have passed the censorship, which was very particular about changes in the diplomatic service. And " the more I heard from Berlin, the clearer it became to me that I was somehow involved in the February crisis ". He felt " outraged by the treatment " meted out to him, and " embittered by the indignity " he had suffered. (But wrongs and slights are a recurrent theme of his autobiography — three or four suffered in his diplomatic career are related in the book.) In Singapore an inquiry reached him from the German Foreign Office " whether his health would allow him to take over another post ". He had not meant to do so, but now feeling " offended in his honour " and in need of amends, he replied that he would. " That it would perhaps have done me more honour not to serve

Hitler's Government was a thought which did not as yet occur to me" (again an admission cleaner than the farrago talked by some other German ex-diplomatists). At last, during a fortnight's stay in Egypt, he learnt that he had been appointed Ambassador in London. "Personally I was a Westerner . . .", he writes. He arrived in Berlin on April 12 (in his "Memorandum", on the 10th). According to Erich Kordt, at that time *chef de cabinet* to Ribbentrop, Dirksen owed his London appointment to Hitler's friendship with Dirksen's stepmother,[1] about whom Dirksen speaks in *Zwischenbilanz* with the bitterest hostility.

The chapter on London is much fuller than that on Tokyo: Dirksen was able to refer to his papers published by the Soviet Government (though not yet to the German documents published by the Western Allies). In fact, what the reader is offered is a rehash of those papers, reshuffled to produce new permutations, diluted with unimportant reminiscences, and seasoned with howlers. But far more interesting than additions are timely omissions, and the change of tone, even as from the "Memorandum" which Dirksen had written for his own record in September 1939. Remarks about the hostility of the regular British diplomatists to Germany have vanished; Hitler is blamed for brushing aside the offer of colonies made through Henderson on March 3, 1938, which in the "Memorandum" was described as "very incomplete and inadequate"; and a rebuke is gone which Dirksen claimed to have administered, apparently in February 1939, to Lord Halifax about Ribbentrop.[2] And here is another example. Dirksen wrote in his "Memorandum":

[1] *Nicht aus den Akten . . .*, page 199: ". . . da Hitler mit der Stiefmutter Dirksens eng befreundet war, glaubte Ribbentrop, dass ihm die Ernennung genehm sein werde". About the part she played in the Nazi era, see Ellisabetta Cerutti, *Ambassador's Wife*, pages 165-8.

[2] Cf. *Dirksen Papers*, page 166, with *Moskau, Tokio, London*, page 239.

> This inflammatory campaign reached its peak in the early days of July, when week-end reports from Warsaw regarding a Danzig-Polish crisis, an ultimatum, &c., provoked a regular feeling of panic and crisis in London. The Embassy soon traced the crisis-mongers: they were American circles working through the American Embassy in Warsaw. This was the first, but very distinct, sign that Roosevelt was interested in an aggravation of the situation, or in war, in order to secure, first the repeal of the neutrality law, and then his re-election thanks to the war.

But now he writes:

> . . . In the first days of July [1939] a short but violent crisis shook the world, when American Press reports announced that Hitler was about to attack Poland and Danzig.

Another thing which has faded out in Dirksen's last book is all anti-Jewish feeling. *Zwischenbilanz* was outspokenly anti-Semitic. " I was proud of my purely Germanic blood long before the theories and doctrines were known which now [in 1935] are common property "; and his father was proud of having been ennobled (*geadelt*) in 1887, " before a whole batch of more or less Jew-tainted families (*angejüdelter Familien*) was ennobled by the liberalistic Emperor Frederick III ". Dirksen further blames William II for admitting Jews into society. Clearly he is entitled to his views — but why change them so suddenly and radically? In his " Memorandum " he explained how, during the confused weeks after Munich, he had tried

> to keep things even till a clarification on a broader basis was forthcoming.
>
> This came very soon in connexion with the anti-Jewish demonstrations in Germany on November 10. They produced an extremely strong reaction in England, partly based on emotion and inadequate

> understanding of the German point of view, and partly deliberately fostered. All the anti-German and pro-Jewish elements went into action and unleashed an unbridled anti-German propaganda — especially the *émigrés*, the influential part of the political and business public who are dependent on the Jews, the ultra-pacifists, &c. Numerous official persons took up a hostile attitude toward us in speeches and public utterances. The Lord Baldwin Fund, with its collections, advertisements, &c., provided another desired opportunity for anti-German propaganda, under a humanitarian guise. During these weeks all voices of reason and all promptings toward mutual clarification were silenced.

But here is the same story as it appears in *Moskau, Tokio, London*:

> I had to limit myself to keeping things even till a clarification on a broader basis was forthcoming.
>
> That clarification came in a terrifying form through the anti-Jewish persecutions enacted by Goebbels on November 10. . . . The disgraceful performance of that day — burning of synagogues, lootings, and ill-treatments — produced throughout Europe a wave of loathing and indignation which silenced all talks.

And elsewhere he writes: " Never in all my life did I feel such shame ". Apparently the one thing which survives from 1939 in the views of the transformed Dirksen is an exaggerated estimate of the influence or importance of the Jews.

The story of Chamberlain's last attempt to reach an understanding with Hitler, in Sir Horace Wilson's talks with Wohlthat at the end of July and with Dirksen on August 3, 1939,[1] is retold in a slovenly summary. The concluding personal part alone now appears in greater detail: and it makes a funny tale.

[1] Analysed in my book, *Europe in Decay* (1950), pages 222-7.

> It was clear to me that only a personal *exposé* in Berlin might, perhaps in cooperation with Wohlthat, have a chance of adding some weight to my reports.

Dirksen left London on August 10. In view of the gravity of the situation and the alleged importance of the offer which had hung fire for nearly three weeks, one would have expected him to go home post-haste. " In Berlin I arrived on a Monday, which must have been August 13." Monday was August 14. When attention was previously called to these dates,[1] Dirksen explained to an English friend that he stopped on his way two days at Bruges to visit the Memling Exhibition — " besides it would not have made sense to arrive in Berlin on a Saturday afternoon ". In fact, it would have been a Friday ; and anyhow the German Foreign Office could hardly have shut down during the week-end of Ciano's visit to Salzburg and Berchtesgaden. Having arrived on the 14th, Dirksen asked Ribbentrop's secretaries to fix up an interview with him, and also to apply for one with Hitler ; and Weizsäcker specially wrote to Ribbentrop urging him to see Dirksen.

" In the next few days (*in den nächsten Tagen*) " Dirksen called on General Halder, C.G.S., and on the Italian Ambassador, Attolico. And again :

> in the next few days no answer to my inquiry was received from the Foreign Minister. It was clear that he did not want to see me. . . . I retired to Gröditzberg [Dirksen's country house in Silesia] to await further developments. But before leaving I called on the chief of the Personnel Department, Kriebel, and told him that in existing circumstances I did not care to be re-employed in the diplomatic service. . . .

And in the " Memorandum " Dirksen writes : " I left for Gröditzberg on August 16 ". Thus he arrived in Berlin

[1] See *Europe in Decay*, page 227.

on the 14th; his interviews with Halder and Attolico can be proved to have been on the 15th; and he left Berlin on the 16th. But where is to be fitted in that long waiting of the " next few days " before and again after those two visits, which made Dirksen, convinced though he was of the vital importance of his seeing Hitler and Ribbentrop, give up the quest in despair and disgust? The story does not make sense.

Dirksen, in his peroration rightly accuses Hitler and Ribbentrop of having, in unleashing the war, shown a " criminal lack of conscience, which — to talk their own jargon — was *einmalig* "; and forgets that once he, too, made that " jargon " his own. But at least Dirksen never claims to have conspired against Hitler, nor asks for recognition on that score.

ERNST VON WEIZSÄCKER

DURING the five crucial years, 1938–1943, Ernst Freiherr von Weizsäcker held the key-position of State Secretary in the German Foreign Office, equivalent to our Permanent Under-Secretary. Although German foreign policy was determined by Hitler, its execution, in spite of occasional deflection into extraneous channels, rested mainly with the regular officials, especially under a Minister like Ribbentrop. Incompetent and lazy, hardly capable of drafting a coherent letter, and concerned with his own advancement, he hung about Hitler's ante-room and neglected his Office, leaving its direction and work to Weizsäcker, who supplied Nazi diplomacy with a civilized façade and a shrewder technique.

At Nuremberg, Erich Kordt, a well-qualified witness, testified to Weizsäcker's " reputation of being the most efficient official in the service ", who managed to establish " a personal hold over the normal activities of the Foreign Office ". But about these little is to be learnt from Weizsäcker's *Memoirs* (until collated with the captured German documents) — they are a laboured yet frantic apologia devoid of real contents, which may impress the uninformed, uncritical reader, but which crumbles when tested. Egocentric as such an apologia is bound to be, it turns the light on to Weizsäcker's personality, and first illumines a blank : but below that polished, well-shaped surface, a wary, anxious man can be discerned ; soft, polite, and without strong convictions ; not a fighter, and conscious of it ; and, like his countryman the Swabian peasant, crafty and naïve. Coulondre speaks of *la façon enveloppée* in which Weizsäcker used to express himself; even more involved is his written argument. Yet adroit though he is, by overdoing his part he defeats his purpose: the rôle of fervent and single-minded worker for peace and amity between nations ill fits the German Nationalist. Weizsäcker cannot altogether obliterate or reinterpret the work he did for Hitler, nor disguise the rancour he feels against those who twice defeated his Germany; and he hardly cares to conceal his bitter dislike of the Czechs and Poles.

Born in 1882, Weizsäcker spent the first part of his active life (1900–1920) in the Imperial Navy, and the second (1920–1945) in the diplomatic service; but his historical discourses suggest a provincial *Gymnasial-Lehrer* of middling intelligence. The German fleet was preparing itself for a " tournament ", not for war against Britain (which Weizsäcker never heard invoked in officers' messes); Tirpitz, a poor orator, went in for long-term naval programs to escape annual debates; and nothing would have pleased the Emperor better than an understanding with Britain. German foreign policy was clumsy, that of the Entente set on war. Weizsäcker charges Sir Edward Grey with *dolus eventualis* — whatever that may mean — and repeats the falsehood that in 1912 Grey had assumed " secret commitments ". At Versailles the German delegation worked hard, without " material " results (the recovery of half Upper Silesia being obviously " immaterial "); and Weizsäcker twice asserts that it was the deliberate aim of the Versailles Treaty to create " permanent discord " between Germany and Poland: an infamous accusation against men, some pro-German, who laboured to find a fair and viable solution. With familiar self-righteousness and self-pity, Weizsäcker wrote in 1944:

> We Germans are not destined patiently to build our house, bit by bit, and then enjoy in peace the

> fruit of our labours. Again and again other Powers have attempted to re-arrange Europe by creating a political vacuum in Germany. . . .

One may well ask who ever disturbed the peace of Bismarck's Prussia, or of the Second or Third Reich. But there is method in Weizsäcker's confusion: Germany's innocence and the guilt of the Allies have to be established.

Weizsäcker's interest turned early to the "League of Nations idea": "national States with unrestricted sovereignty seemed to me out of date". But, in his account, on devilry at Versailles followed hypocrisy at Geneva. "I left my Geneva post more impatient of foreign pretensions than I was when I came." "My memories of the League of Nations are rather bitter, and my criticism may seem passionate." "In five years [1927–1932] I saw no one rise to the surface at Geneva who deserved being called a statesman"; Briand and Stresemann thought in terms of parliamentary oratory; and at Locarno Germany was made to pay an excessive price for admission to the comity of nations. "I was later told that Stresemann valued the work I did at Geneva. I myself had not noticed it and rather avoided his company. . . ." He praises Stresemann's successor, Curtius, for "better husbanding Germany's economic and political resources", and for being less "large-hearted (*grosszügig*)"; and he records with satisfaction the "close cooperation" between Germans and Bolsheviks, which "irked" Lord Cecil. Rapallo appealed to Weizsäcker more than Locarno. French diplomatists he reproaches with "a memory too good for their profession": whatever the Germans do when victorious must instantly be forgotten when they suffer defeat. With acrimonious resentment he disparages the very substantial concessions to Germany in the post-Locarno period, of which the momentum continued to grow even after 1933 (when preventive action would have been both appropriate and easy); he was, in fact, one of those German Nationalists whose carping criticism of the "fulfilment policy" helped to pave the way for Hitler. "Friends of neutral nationality", he admits, "have reproached me with being not free myself from the nationalism which the Germans developed in the League." But what he now detects in the "exciting and instructive" years 1918–1933 is "the foreign contribution to the infection" of the "German fever" during the Hitler period: the Allies must be made co-responsible for that criminal régime which Weizsäcker himself served from its inception till its collapse.

He now tries to explain why he did so — on the average once in every five or six pages: in 290 pages he tells some twenty times of his inner struggles and hesitations, and asserts more than thirty times that his sole purpose was the preservation of peace. In June 1832, Heine wrote about Lafayette participating in riots "with the good intention by his presence to restrain the people from the worst excesses":

> He resembles the tutor who accompanied the pupil in his charge to brothels so that he should not get drunk, and next to pubs that at least he should not gamble, and to gambling-houses to preserve him from duels — but when it came to a duel, good and proper, the old fellow acted as his second.

A fitting text for Weizsäcker's story.

January 1933 found him Minister to Norway. "I had to ask myself whether it was right for me to collaborate", which implied concessions to the new German "style in thought and speech". He repeatedly discussed the question with German colleagues, always reaching the same result: "to quit would be desertion"; "to stand aside" and leave the field to dangerous amateurs "would be senseless"; "the Third Reich cannot last". June 30, 1934, made him waver — but it held out hope:

the Nazis had started killing each other. In June 1936 he was recalled to the Foreign Office as Political Director. This led to further searchings of heart — but then work at headquarters would show whether there was a chance of a policy of peace at home and abroad. Before starting for Berlin, the provident Weizsäcker told an intimate friend that

> afterwards it would look as if I had actively collaborated, but I had to take that odium upon myself with the sole aim of perhaps preserving peace.

In the winter of 1936–1937 he was torn by conflicting emotions — " to leave would be to desert the flag ", but to stay would be useless if the course was set for war. " A new era must open in foreign policy. The Foreign Office must regain control, &c." He could not refuse co-operation.

In the purge and reshuffle of February 1938 Weizsäcker was offered the State Secretaryship.

> To refuse the post and leave it to I knew not whom would have meant consciously to shirk responsibility. . . . The primary duty of the Foreign Office was to fight for peace, for world peace. . . . I decided to take that struggle upon myself.

On March 5, 1938, after a talk with Ribbentrop, Weizsäcker claims to have recorded:

> It is Ribbentrop's changeable outlook which makes me think there is a chance of preventing war, the only task for which I take this cross upon myself.

And now he writes:

> A strange existence started for me in the spring of 1938. . . . Day and night I kept watch like a guard on the coast who fears lest wild, foaming waves might somewhere wash over the dyke. It was my first task to get the new Foreign Minister to join the crew manning the dyke.

The reader rubs his eyes. What? Ribbentrop a guardian of peace? Weizsäcker professes not to have discovered till the summer of 1938 that "it was practically useless" to argue with him about politics. Erich Kordt was Weizsäcker's "closest confidant in the Office"; he was liaison between Ribbentrop and the Foreign Office, 1934–1936, and his First Secretary at the London Embassy, 1936–1938; "I always unreservedly told Weizsäcker my opinion about Ribbentrop", writes Kordt; but Weizsäcker had still to learn what kind of man he was. Who accepts this will believe anything.

On May 22, 1938, Weizsäcker recorded:

> I was very rude to Ribbentrop to-day when he said that we ought to provoke the Czechs. "I must most categorically contradict you", I roared at him (*brüllte ich ihn an*) at the Tempelhof aerodrome.

The noise of engines presumably offered an opportunity for roaring.

Herr von Weizsäcker was a very cautious man. He must not be judged by anything he said, wrote, or even did under the Nazi régime. His minutes of conversations were "adjusted to the mentality of their readers", and he used language calculated "to produce the desired effect" — "a great deal of irony was in it". Those engaged in the politics of Hitler-Germany "spoke and wrote for pathological types in competition with pathological types (*Psychopathen*)". About a private note in which, he referred to his own side, quite naturally, as "we", he now remarks: "This note was worded in such a way that it could safely fall into wrong German hands — as in general almost all my private notes during the Hitler period". He must not be judged even by his private letters, in which appropriate statements were inserted to mislead the censor: "They, too, should be read with as much caution as official reports, directives, &c." In short, a past master in camouflage. Then only?

There can be no doubt that Weizsäcker did not enjoy the life of those years. He must have loathed working for, with, and under the Nazis; he could not have relished their company, methods, or manners, the noise of their mass-meetings and the hysteria of their leaders. But he seems to have lacked the courage and resolution to break with them. And so he was drawn into the maelstrom. Moreover, a sincere German Nationalist he was prepared, like so many of them, to serve Hitler loyally so long as Hitler seemed to be realizing safely and efficiently nationalist aims. Germany's rearmament, the *Anschluss*, and the annexation of the Sudetenland, the recovery of Memel, Danzig, the Corridor, Upper Silesia, and at least of parts of Posnania, the inclusion of a " rump-Czechia " and a " rump-Poland " in the German sphere, a resurrection of German power in Europe, these were also Weizsäcker's aims, to be realized by steady, well-considered steps. It was not war as such that he abhorred, but a war in which Germany risked being defeated a second time. He was convinced that the Western Powers would fight rather than deliver Czechoslovakia into German hands; and in 1938 the German Army Command saw no chance for Germany in such a war. Hence Weizsäcker, while trying to garner the gains of German blackmail, was appalled by the risks which Hitler incurred before Munich. Indeed, Weizsäcker stood for peace, peace at any price — to be paid by the other side. And in the pursuit of the price he was not squeamish about methods.

Here is an example.[1] During the *Anschluss*, March 11-12, 1938, the German Government, to keep the Czechs quiet, lavished on them effusively cordial assurances; and on the 14th, with German consent, Chamberlain informed

[1] See *Documents on British Foreign Policy; 1919–1939*, Third Series, vol. i, nos. 79 and 83; and *Documents on German Foreign Policy, 1918–1945*, Series D, vol. ii, nos. 72-4, 80, 81, 85, 88, 90, 99, and 101.

Parliament of Göring's declaration, " expressly renewed later on behalf of Herr Hitler, that it would be the earnest endeavour of the German Government to improve German-Czech relations ", and that, in particular, the German troops had orders to keep away from the Czech frontier; and of Neurath's assurance " that Germany considered herself bound by the German-Czechoslovak Arbitration Convention of October, 1925 ". (" By these assurances, solemnly given and more than once repeated," declared Halifax, " we naturally expect the German Government to abide.") But this passage in Chamberlain's speech was deleted by the German Press; and when the crisis was over, on March 21, the German Foreign Office explained to their Minister in Budapest, in a telegram of which the draft was initialed by Weizsäcker:

> The Field Marshal's assurances referred exclusively to *ad hoc* measures connected with carrying out action in Austria by which Czechoslovakia would not be affected.

To the London Embassy the point was put in a more enveloped manner:

> The impression seems to have been created in official circles . . . abroad that . . . assurances were given . . . in respect of the integrity of Czechoslovakia. . . .
>
> For your information, and if necessary as directive for language to be held, I would mention that . . . nothing was said on German side other than assurance that on occasion of military action in Austria Czechoslovak frontier would be respected in every way. . . . Beyond that only active desire for an improvement in German-Czechoslovak relations was expressed and . . . reference was made by Herr von Neurath to the existence of the German-Czechoslovak Arbitration Treaty of 1925.

That Weizsäcker approved of this contorted interpretation, which admitted the words and deprived them of their meaning, is shown by a contemporary directive ; and that he was at least a willing party to that dishonest procedure, by his treatment of the matter in his *Memoirs* :

> At the time of the *Anschluss* assurances were given to the Czech Minister in Berlin that the military action would not affect his country. In Prague and Paris an attempt was made to represent the communication made through Göring and Neurath as a renunciation of ever-exerting influence [with regard to the Sudetenland] (*als einen dauernd gültigen Verzicht auf Einflussnahme*).

Thus he limits the assurances to the single event ; speaks of Prague and Paris, and omits London ; misrepresents the Allied interpretation of the German assurances ; and suppresses the reference to the Arbitration Treaty, which in itself showed that the impression of permanency was intended.

The handling of that treaty forms another shady chapter in German diplomatic history.[1] Concluded at Locarno, it was left unaffected when the main Locarno treaties were scrapped by the Germans. But on February 5, 1938, Neurath informed the German Minister in Prague that, while in March 1936 it was decided to treat the Arbitration agreement as " continuing in force " (to avoid " unnecessarily enlarging the circle of problems raised by our Rhineland action "), and its denunciation was not contemplated even now (as this might suggest " active plans against Czechoslovakia "), further acknowledgment of its validity should be avoided, and, if occasion arose, he should give it as his own opinion that " owing to the collapse of the League of Nations, treaties such as the German-Czechoslovak Treaty of Arbitration have lost

[1] See *Documents and Materials relating to the Eve of the Second World War*, published by the Ministry of Foreign Affairs of the U.S.S.R., vol. i, no. 2; and German *Documents*, nos. 34, 38, 73, 78, 80, 84, 268, and 269.

their political foundation". Five weeks later, to reassure the Czechs, the Arbitration Treaty was cited once more. But on June 25, 1938, Neurath's instructions of February 5 were renewed by Weizsäcker. He had his full share in slippery transactions.

Weizsäcker knew of Hitler's decision to destroy Czechoslovakia, and of his instructions to the Sudetens always to ask for more than the Czechs could concede. Therefore, whatever their concessions, he continued acrimoniously to discourse on Czech intransigence and provocations, and on the ineffectiveness of British interventions in Prague. He tried to promote a "chemical process of disruption of the Czechoslovak political structure", and expected it surely and safely to achieve Germany's aim; whereas "mechanical aid", that is, the use of force, would bring about intervention by the Western Powers. Weizsäcker's contention that he opposed war in 1938 is borne out by the German documents, and was accepted by the Nuremberg Tribunal. His reasoning is set forth in his memorandum of June 20, 1938.[1] German aims in the East, he wrote, can only be attained if unopposed by the Entente.

> We have no military recipe for defeating France and Britain. . . . The war would . . . end with our exhaustion and defeat. . . . Therefore the task of German diplomacy is clearly to ascertain the limits to which German policy can be pushed . . . without causing the Entente to intervene.

They might abandon Czechoslovakia to her doom if brought about by "internal disruptive tendencies", and not by "direct attacks from abroad".

> This process must, however, be a gradual one and must aim, by plebiscites and amputation of districts, at a collapse of the remaining area . . . Germany . . . is in a position to organize the desired development . . .

[1] *G.D.* no. 259.

— which would also seal " the ultimate fate of the rump of Czechoslovakia ". Moreover such procedure is advisable " because of our relations with Poland ": " once the Czech question is settled, it is generally taken for granted that Poland is next on the list "; but premature alarm should be avoided. Thus Weizsäcker readily envisaged even further schemes of German expansion provided no excessive risks were incurred.

At the end of July, Ribbentrop proposed to enjoin on German diplomatists clear and firm language about Czechoslovakia and about Germany's readiness to risk and win a war against the Western Powers. Weizsäcker demurred.

> I remarked [he writes in a minute of July 21, 1938] that it was necessary to speak to third parties in such a way as to obtain credence. And if it was our business to fool foreign countries,[1] it was nevertheless our duty not to dupe one another. I did not believe that we should win this war.

And then, early in August, Ribbentrop decided to declare in a circular to German Missions abroad that the Western Powers would not intervene in a German-Czech conflict, but if they did would suffer a crushing defeat. " I argued in speaking and writing ", claims Weizsäcker in his *Memoirs*, that

> the circular was not likely to convince our Missions. Their chiefs would believe the thickly laid on arguments as little as I did. . . . Herr von Ribbentrop may prescribe to his Ambassadors what language to hold; but should refrain from trying to make dunces of them (*sie zu verdummen*).

The reader may well wonder at Weizsäcker's boldness in thus talking to Ribbentrop: but then these two minutes[2] were for his own eye and use only. There are photographs

[1] These last ten words are omitted in the *Memoirs*.

[2] *Ibid.* nos. 304 and 331.

of both in our Foreign Office Library: they are unsigned, and bear no mark of having been communicated to, or read by, anyone.

Sir Nevile Henderson, who returned from London on August 31, spoke to Weizsäcker about the importance of the next few days

> for the peaceful settlement of the Sudeten problem. . . . It was a question of forcing the unreliable Beneš to make a comprehensive offer to Henlein and tying him down to a public statement, so that he could no longer evade the issue. . . . Sir Nevile did not fail to make disapproving remarks about Beneš's methods.

That such was Henderson's language seems confirmed by his own report to London.[1] No wonder then that Weizsäcker ascribes to him " much common sense and tact ", and " too much intelligence always to side with the Czechs ". Indeed, provided Germany eschewed violence, Henderson " gave us his support " in the Sudeten question. To London he did not pass on even half of what Ribbentrop said to him (an assertion again borne out by a study of Henderson's reports); " the effect would have been too alarming ". Weizsäcker approvingly quotes from Donosti's *Mussolini e l' Europa* a passage about " the triangle Attolico-Henderson-Weizsäcker ":

> They long worked together with such mutual trust that, one might say, they forgot that they belonged to different nations. Conscious of the higher interests of their countries, they knew when to preserve silence toward their own chiefs, or to arrange between themselves what to say to them in order to direct them on to the path favourable to peace.

Weizsäcker obviously sees nothing peculiar in the suggestion that Henderson had to treat Chamberlain and Halifax as Attolico and himself treated Mussolini and Ciano,

[1] *G.D.* vol. ii, no. 419, and *B.D.* vol. ii, no. 736.

Hitler and Ribbentrop. As for the "mutual trust": while the German documents abound with Henderson's disastrous "confidences", none from Weizsäcker to Henderson appears in the British. "Henderson had too much tact to quote me in telegrams of an indiscreet character", writes Weizsäcker; and in reading the British Blue Book he saw how careful Henderson had been not to compromise him. But need such "tact" have extended to dispatches, and especially to Henderson's private letters to Halifax? The warnings of Captain von Albedyl, acting Chief of the Attaché-Group, were duly transmitted by Henderson or his staff.[1]

Weizsäcker claims to have been cognizant of pre-Munich military plotting against Hitler — he himself would have been a mere spectator: "I was wont to say that we could not shoot with our Foreign Office files". And on a later occasion, to Erich Kordt: "Have you a man with a pistol? I regret, it was not part of my education to kill a man." He also, distantly, approved of the step undertaken by Erich Kordt, through his brother, Theo, Counsellor of the Embassy in London, "to inform Halifax and Chamberlain of Hitler's real intentions" — the British were thought in need of "waking up".

> The purpose of that step was to urge the British Government to continue as hitherto to press for a peaceful settlement of the Sudeten question but veto in unambiguous language any resort to force: Hitler would draw back.

The story of that singular *démarche* (September 7) is told in Erich Kordt's book, *Nicht aus den Akten.*[2]

> If asked [writes Kordt] my brother was to confirm that his instructions had come through me, which, in view of the known close connexion between State

[1] *B.D.*, Enclosures in nos. 575 and 714.

[2] See below, pages 92-4.

> Secretary Weizsäcker and myself, implied that the step had his approval.[1]

A few days earlier, Weizsäcker had a talk with the League High Commissioner for Danzig, a Swiss, Carl Burckhardt, who repeated its gist to the British Minister in Berne and to a British diplomatist at Geneva.[2] Weizsäcker, anonymous in both, told Burckhardt about the aggressive mood of Hitler, who was convinced that the Western Powers would not fight. The only method to make him see the truth, thought Weizsäcker,

> would be a personal letter from the Prime Minister showing that if an attack were made by Germany on Czechoslovakia, a war would start in which Great Britain would inevitably be on the opposite side to Germany. . . .
>
> Burckhardt's interlocutor said he could not obviously suggest that to H.M. Ambassador. He had therefore taken the course of asking him, Burckhardt, to act as intermediary. . . .

On September 9 — as appears from the British *Documents* — Henderson was instructed to give a new warning to Hitler; but he demurred: "all are convinced" that such a *démarche* "is likely to be fatal to prospects of peace". The suggestion was thus scotched by the trusty British member of the "triangle", apparently ignorant of its origin.[3]

About the nature and purpose of the *démarche* solicited from the British Government, a marked discrepancy appears between Weizsäcker and Kordt. Kordt states that Weizsäcker, Canaris, Beck, and Halder all desired a

[1] Erich Kordt, when asked at Nuremberg whether his brother did "disclose that State Secretary Weizsäcker was involved", replied: "I can't tell you. I don't know. You'd better ask my brother." (Weizsäcker Trial, June 4, 1948, page 7465.)

[2] *B.D.* vol. ii, no. 775, and Appendix IV, pages 689-92.

[3] *B.D.* nos. 815, 819, 823, and 825.

public declaration which would have disclosed the danger to the German people and Army, and thereby justified a *coup* against Hitler;[1] while Weizsäcker claims that he was against a public warning " because it might too much encourage the Czechs ". Weizsäcker wished for Munich, and now celebrates it, in pacifist terms, as his own achievement:

> . . . the day of Munich was the last happy day of my life. War was avoided. . . . My conscience told me in Munich that my sacrifice, of serving as State Secretary in the Foreign Office under such uncontrollable conditions, was justified.

In the same breath he claims to have wished and worked for Hitler's downfall, and to have secured for him a victory which, in Weizsäcker's own words, made Hitler appear to the Germans as " a sort of magician ".

Weizsäcker gives a patently disingenuous account of his own part in the final " collapse of the remaining area " of Czechoslovakia, which he himself had set as aim to German diplomacy more than three months before Munich. After Munich, feeling that there was no danger of foreign intervention on behalf of Czechoslovakia, he watched her final destruction with complacency, if not approval. But at his trial he explained the absence of German " resistance " to it by the indifference of foreign Powers, for which he seems to blame them in his *Memoirs*:

> The Western Powers . . . were not prepared to aid Prague. This was obvious in a talk I had with the British Ambassador on March 12 or 13 [really the 14th]: Henderson emphasized that the German interest was predominant in the Czech area. Still more explicit was Chamberlain three days later in the House of Commons when, unmoved, he dropped Czechia.

[1] See *Nicht aus den Akten*, page 244.

Apparently to pay ransom to the Germans may even give satisfaction to reasonable people: over the "retrocession of Memel", the Lithuanian Foreign Minister,

> *ein sympathischer Mann*, himself seemed relieved and content. Had the Great Powers objected . . . they would no doubt have brought the fact to our notice.

The *Völkischer Beobachter*, for one, noticed with indignation what Sir Samuel Hoare said on the subject in the House of Commons on March 22.

In 1939 Weizsäcker fulminated against the British guarantee to Poland (it disturbed his programme of *Zermürbungspolitik* — grinding technique — which was to "make the Poles more amenable"): "a blank cheque" for her Government, he called it, and a free rein for subordinate Polish officials to oppress the *Volksdeutsche*. Nor could such a guarantee intimidate Hitler — "how could it be believed in London", he now writes, "that it would serve the cause of peace?" But Weizsäcker claims it to have been his own aim "to discourage and restrain both Hitler and the Poles". On May 30 he was glad to engage in an exploratory talk with the Russian Chargé d'Affaires—

> throughout the Nazi period I could not see why we left axiomatic hostility between us and Russia as a basic asset to the policy of our numerous opponents. . . . The prospect was alluring, harried as we now were (*in unserer jetzt bedrängten Lage*), to correct that mistake. To attempt a *détente* with Russia was to make real foreign policy, and to work for peace, completely ignoring domestic ideologies.

The reader will again rub his eyes. What? Nazi Germany was *bedrängt* — harried, set upon, pummelled — in May 1939? And a German-Russian *rapprochement* was a move favourable to peace? It would "cool down Polish hotheads", Weizsäcker professes to have thought, and would stop Hitler from coveting Russian territory, and also Polish territory " so long as he was not altogether certain of Moscow's attitude ". Yet on May 6, before anything was happening, Göring's right-hand man, General Bodenschatz, had warned the French " that something was brewing in the East ", and had foretold a Fourth Partition of Poland. On the 9th, Coulondre reported a Berlin rumour of such an offer to Russia. But no such thoughts disturbed Weizsäcker's gladness on May 30 — though he admits, as an inconsequential afterthought, that Hitler's " originally defensive intentions might change in the end into an aggressive plan ", and that " his renunciation of hostility to Russia " might imply " a risk to peace ". Does Weizsäcker seriously expect the reader to accept that he believed then, and even when writing his book, that Hitler, in approaching Russia, was moved by " originally defensive intentions " ? Again, who accepts this will believe anything.

Later on, Weizsäcker claims to have sounded the tocsin: to have warned Britain in June through the Kordts that Hitler might outbid her in Moscow; and on August 15 he told Henderson that Russia would hardly help the Poles, but " would in the end join in sharing in the Polish spoils ". But so did Göring — in May through Bodenschatz, and on August 7 personally at a meeting with British business men in Slesvig. Once more there were two policies: one, by the threat of Russia to achieve a second Munich; the other, through an agreement with Russia to deter the Western Powers from defending Poland. If neo-Munichry is to count for merit, Göring, instead of a death verdict, should have received a few more decorations.

The style of conducting negotiations with the " Polish hotheads ", the reader could hardly gather from Weizsäcker's *Memoirs*. But here is an example. Since June the question of some additional customs officials or frontier guards, sent by Poland to check the smuggling of arms into Danzig, had been blowing up into a major affair. On August 18 the Poles showed readiness to yield. Thereupon the following plan was submitted to Berlin.

> Gauleiter Forster intends to extend claims . . . to about 50 Polish customs officials and their immediate withdrawal. Should the Poles yield again, it is intended to increase the claims further in order to make accord impossible. . . .

Weizsäcker approved, but added that

> discussions will have to be conducted and pressure exerted in such a way that responsibility for failure to come to an agreement and the consequences rests with Poland.

The suggestion was readily adopted, and on the 22nd Weizsäcker was assured that negotiations would " end in a complete deadlock ", and the Poles " be blamed for it " ; and the next morning, that " about 6 P.M. negotiations will be declared to have failed through the fault of the Poles ".[1]

Equally brazen and more insidious was the undelivered German Note of August 30, which Ribbentrop " gabbled " to Henderson that night, and which was broadcast on the 31st, at 9 P.M., some eight hours before the invasion of Poland. Weizsäcker now boasts of his share in drafting it, and calls it " a reasonable compromise plan, the first constructive idea for months ". In reality it was a close replica of Munich : with the Corridor in place of Sudetenland, and a new plebiscite under an International Commission (Weizsäcker had presided over the previous Commission, and after a few days even Henderson wrote on October 6, 1938 : " I never want to work with Germans again "). So Weizsäcker was at his

[1] NG-2172, 3615, and 1992 : presented at Weizsäcker's trial at Nuremberg on January 13, 1948.

old game: "chemical" disintegration and *Zermürbung*, "plebiscites and amputation of districts", and a collapse of the rest or rump. But whom did he expect to fool when writing his book?

On September 5, 1939, Weizsäcker wrote a diary-note which was produced at his trial, and now appears in his *Memoirs*:

> The entire sense of my work since April 1938 was to contribute my utmost to the preservation of peace. What I did I mostly could not write down. In the first five or six months I tried to attain my aim mainly by the direct means of giving my views to Herr von Ribbentrop. Later on, better acquainted with his mentality, I preferred other means. . . .

Thus the cautious Weizsäcker put down on paper a highly compromising statement which could serve no purpose but that of an alibi in changed circumstances: another form of caution. And next follows a barrage of peace invocations — here are four from seven pages:

> To restore peace, this was from the first day of war the sense of my work. . . . I was for peace, no matter at all on what basis. . . . What was to be done? To keep still, localize the war, preserve the neutrality of the neutrals, promote moves for peace approaches. . . . Peace was my only concern. . . .

Weizsäcker grieved over the Russo-Finnish war, and rejoiced when it was over. "Somewhere at least shooting had stopped." But in between occurs this significant passage:

> England and France seemed inclined to come to the support of the Finns, and in doing so to cut off Germany's access to the Scandinavian ores. After lengthy hesitations, they inquired in Oslo and Stockholm if Norway and Sweden would permit the passage of troops. In the end a few crocodile tears was all they accorded to the Finns, when these, after a brave defence . . . concluded an armistice.

> What a different course the Second World War would have taken if British and French contingents had gone to fight on the Finnish side against Soviet Russia!

Yes, indeed: Hitler might have won it. And for once that passionate peace-lover, Weizsäcker, does not recoil from "an extension of bloodshed" — but then the blood would not have been German, and the extension could only have benefited Germany. (As for the strangely misattributed "crocodile tears", they are an example of the well-nigh automatic *médisance* of this high-minded man.) Similarly, if only Mussolini and Hitler had left the Balkans alone, it might

> have given a free run to Russian ambitions toward the Mediterranean, brought them into stronger conflict with British interests, and thus produced a completely different alignment of Powers in the East.

But when it was Germany which stood on the brink of war with Russia, Weizsäcker wrote to Ribbentrop on April 28, 1941:[1]

> I can summarize in one sentence my views on a German-Russian conflict: If every Russian city reduced to ashes were as valuable to us as a sunken British warship, I should advocate the German-Russian war for this summer. . . . The sole decisive factor is whether this project will hasten the fall of England. . . .
>
> England is close to collapse . . . Russia is no potential ally of the English. . . . With Russia we do not destroy any English hopes. . . .
>
> A German attack on Russia would only give the British new moral strength.

Weizsäcker's *Memoirs* teem with absurdities, distortions, and untruths fit to deceive only those who wish to be

[1] See *Nazi-Soviet Relations, 1939–1941*, published by the Department of State (1948), page 333.

deceived. Yet one statement of his calls for a categorical denial: he alleges that in July 1940, when " the air was full of peace rumours ", Lord Lothian, then Ambassador in Washington, through a Quaker sought contact with the Germans, " which, considering the ways of British diplomacy, he must have been authorized to do ". Lothian had no such instructions or authorization, and he never made such an approach. The approach was made not by Lothian but to him, and was rejected. Indeed, can anyone honestly believe that in July 1940, in Britain's " finest hour ", Mr. Churchill authorized a " peace approach " to the Germans? or that Halifax did so without Churchill's knowledge? or that Lothian made such an approach unauthorized by his Government? Whatever the origin of that story it is a falsehood.

ERICH AND THEO KORDT

ERICH KORDT, born in December 1903, held at the outbreak of war a comparatively junior post in the German diplomatic service, and if he has an " extra-official " story to tell,[1] this is mainly due to his long association with Ribbentrop, and to some curious transactions which he now delights to relate. Kordt entered the Foreign Ministry in 1928, and from 1931 was employed in the League of Nations and Disarmament Department; next, he was to have been seconded to the League Secretariat, but on Germany's withdrawal from the League, in October 1933, was placed as observer for League affairs at the Berne Legation, under Weizsäcker, then Minister to Switzerland. In April 1934, on Ribbentrop being appointed Commissioner for Disarmament Problems (*Beauftragte der Reichsregierung für Abrüstungsfragen*), Kordt was recalled to Berlin, and attached to him. Theo Kordt was at that time *chef de cabinet* to the State Secretary, von Bülow; and the Political Director of the Foreign Ministry explained to Erich Kordt that, while his previous work on disarmament problems rendered his appointment plausible, his brother's position would make it easy for him " to keep the State Secretary informed about the activities of Ribbentrop who, though placed under the Foreign Ministry, meant to render himself independent ".

Shortly afterwards Ribbentrop went on a special mission to London and Paris, a crisis having arisen over

[1] Erich Kordt, *Nicht aus den Akten . . .*, Union Deutsche Verlagsgesellschaft. Stuttgart.

German rearmament and Barthou's consequent refusal to continue disarmament talks.

> I was strictly enjoined [writes Erich Kordt] in no circumstances to correct Ribbentrop's reports to Berlin. All the folly of the man should clearly appear. Bülow had already discovered that Ribbentrop was incapable of drafting a report in comprehensible German. " The *Reichspräsident* [Hindenburg] should not be allowed to form false ideas about Ribbentrop, nor should Hitler ", were my instructions. Then there will be hope that Ribbentrop's activities will reach an early end. Wherein Bülow was to prove mistaken.

Kordt's connexion with Ribbentrop lasted nearly seven years. The first two covered the period of the disarmament talks, of the Anglo-German Naval Agreement, and of the Rhineland crisis; in 1934 Kordt was Third Secretary, in 1935 Second Secretary, and in 1936 came with Ribbentrop to London as First Secretary to the Embassy; on Ribbentrop being made Foreign Minister, Kordt became his *chef de cabinet*, and held the post from February 1938 till December 1940. He claims to have acted as observer on Ribbentrop rather than as his helpful collaborator. Undoubtedly he saw and heard a good deal, and from the questions or problems set to him by Ribbentrop, could still gauge if not told directly, which way minds were moving. "Almost without any endeavour on my part, circumstances made me the most important source of information for the highest officials of the Foreign Ministry about the plans of the Nazi leaders."

One may well believe that Kordt never was devoted or even loyal to Ribbentrop: but clearly he must have been useful and pliable to advance so quickly and to last so long. Now he would have it believed that he kept away as much as possible from Ribbentrop, and frequently stood up to him, provoking clashes. Asked at Weizsäcker's trial why then Ribbentrop retained him, Kordt replied:

> I have pondered about that and I don't actually know the reason. It may have been the difficulty of replacing me. Generally in the years before 1938 he apologized when we had a clash. But that was, of course, before he became Foreign Minister.

Kordt added that perhaps Ribbentrop "was a little superstitious to quit with somebody whom he thought to have helped him in this thing about the naval treaty". A mascot?

Now he exhibits Ribbentrop. It is indeed difficult to speak about that sinister buffoon without exposing him to ridicule; but Kordt does it with relish, tramping on the stuffed guy who once was his master. In the anecdotes he tells not much is new, nor could it be: for Ribbentrop was repetitive in his inanities, and monotonous in his stupid arrogance, his pretensions, violence, and subserviency. But Kordt appears to find interest and amusement in things which seem trivial or tasteless. Still, his account of Ribbentrop's visits to this country is not without value: even people, who could not have failed to size-up Ribbentrop morally, thought it expedient to cultivate Hitler's envoy, and thereby helped to build up with Hitler the position of one unsurpassed, even among the Nazis, in malignant folly.

Most telling in Kordt's book are the illustrations: Ribbentrop saluting Hitler at the entrance to the Opera, in dress and manner a perfect replica of the cinema commissionaire; Meissner and Ribbentrop talking to Hitler at a gala party, both covered with the tinsel of over-decorated Christmas trees, Meissner standing to attention with thumbs in line with the seam of the trouser, while Ribbentrop hangs on Hitler's lips with an expression of concentrated vacuity. Indeed, a fuller collection of such photographs would make an excellent documentary film of the Third Reich, from which the men who served Hitler in his time but now claim to have been in constant opposition against him should not be omitted.

Erich Kordt in his story of why he served Hitler is a disciple of Weizsäcker, though less subtle and cautious. Kordt, too, repeatedly " hesitated ", but friends urged him to continue ; still, he does not soak the reader with blubbering sham-pacifism, but much rather dwells on his quasi-conspiratorial performances ; and, whatever the significance or value of those performances, at least the two Kordts in their intercourse with Englishmen did not hide, like Weizsäcker, behind a thick curtain. Moreover, Erich Kordt shows more frankness in his appraisal of the situation ; admits the danger which from the outset attached to Hitler's successes even where Germany seemed to benefit — which implies a criticism of those who helped to achieve them ; and he speaks of the insufficiency of the men whose duty it should have been to check Hitler in good time. About the attitude of the German masses he writes :

> The journey [with Hitler in May 1938] was for me in one respect a shattering experience. . . . I saw at close quarters crowds of men and women of all ages at the railway stations pressing towards the carriage. They yelled till their voices broke, and with flushed faces and outstretched arms seemed in the throes of St. Vitus dance. . . . Some women, as it were, flattening their noses against the side of the carriage, held up their children. Hitler would for a moment hold the child's little arms with both hands, and shake them somewhat mechanically, without any change of expression. . . . The happy mothers continued to shout *Heil*. . . .
>
> A middle-aged Berlin woman often came to my mind, who told me that she went to all manner of demonstrations lining the streets through which the

Führer passed, but had never yet properly seen him, for whenever he approached her eyes would fill with tears.

That attitude of the woman in the street, of the workman and the soldier, of German youth and the junior officers, worked even on those who feared the risks which Hitler was taking: so long as he was successful opposition to him was unreal. Had there been the will to overthrow Hitler, the alleged *contretemps* of Chamberlain's journeys to Berchtesgaden and Munich would not have been decisive.

> I often could not rid myself of the feeling [writes Kordt] that, barring a few men who themselves lacked the necessary means and authority, the opposition in the Supreme Army Command, while wishing to have at their disposal an effective apparatus for a *coup d'état*, recoiled from creating it when there was still time. Did they fear being forced to act by the existence of such an apparatus? Looking back, it appears to have been the greatest weakness, nay the tragedy, of the opposition that in this circle there was no impelling personality, no politician or general with the urge to act. . . . Had there but been among us an uninhibited type like Rommel, or a younger, aggressive character like Count Stauffenberg!

Kordt stated at Nuremberg that in September 1938 Weizsäcker " was certainly not against the *Putsch*. Perhaps he doubted a little bit whether, in the end, the generals would follow us." Follow whom? Weizsäcker, the muffled hero, or the 34-year-old secretary of Ribbentrop? And here are Kordt's answers to questions asked by one of the American prosecuting counsel:

> *Q*. In other words, when you made your efforts to have the British follow your advice, Weizsäcker himself doubted whether the generals would, and yet you expected the British Empire to follow this advice?
>
> *A*. Exactly.

Q. And you anticipated . . . that the British Empire would support an alleged movement by some of the high-ranking army generals and members of the S.S., who were unnamed, to foment a revolt? . . .

A. I thought that they ran no risk at all if they followed our advice.

What was that " advice " tendered to H.M. Government which they, so disastrously, failed to follow? What were its background, meaning, and purpose?

Weizsäcker and the Kordts differed little from Hitler or Henlein in their attitude or feelings towards Czechoslovakia; the game of inveighing against Beneš and his people was carried on with zest, and is continued in their memoirs — Kordt, crowing over Beneš's end, tastefully refers to him as *der geprellte Betrüger* (" the cheated cheat "). Partition was to be the fate of Czechoslovakia, and German vassalage of the *Rest-Tschechei* (" rump-Czechia "). But they were convinced that these aims could be attained by gradual steps connived in by the Western Powers, while open German aggression would force these into a war which, they were told by their own Army leaders, Germany was bound to lose: Hitler and Ribbentrop were gambling with her fate just to satisfy their insane passions and vanity.

On May 21, 1938, during the " week-end crisis ", Brauchitsch, Commander-in-Chief of the Army, urgently demanded to see Ribbentrop. After the interview:

" Do you know our real military position? " Ribbentrop said to me [writes Kordt]. ". . . Brauchitsch has just told me that at present we are not able to take on even Czechoslovakia. He says that in almost all arms we are absolutely inferior. If this is true, my policy is completely wrong."

And Kordt adds in another context:

At that time it was hardly disputed that Germany would suffer defeat in a war against the Western

> Powers. It was still possible to talk openly about it with our Nazi rulers.

An exaggerated idea of the Allies' will to resist, and fear of the risks to which Hitler seemed to expose Germany, drove German generals and diplomatists into opposition during the weeks preceding Munich. But neither then nor later were they willing to relinquish Hitler's ill-gotten gains; and in London they cultivated the appeasers rather than the Foreign Office where the German game was too well understood.

On August 23, 1938, Theo Kordt, Chargé d'Affaires in the Ambassador's absence, met Sir Horace Wilson at the house of Mr. F. P. Conwell-Evans, a friend of the Kordts and a prominent member of the Anglo-German Society. Theo Kordt's official report [1] of the interview shows him conducting it on orthodox Nazi lines: he discoursed about the "week-end crisis" and Germany's injured innocence; and when discussing the Runciman Mission, recited the usual tale that Czechoslovakia

> would refuse to make the necessary concessions as long as she definitely believed that she could count on support from both Western Powers in any eventuality. . . .

An artificial French creation, she was now "like an air-cushion from which the air was gradually escaping". Her "ties with Soviet Russia and France must cease": her place was not with Germany's opponents but with her friends. Horace Wilson "listened with great attention"; thought that such a policy could be discussed but must not be imposed by force; and agreed that the position of Czechoslovakia was "unnatural and absurd". It would be the height of folly for Britain and Germany to fight each other; he favoured a "large-scale" German policy in South-Eastern Europe, and did not fear her using "its

[1] *G.D.* ii, no. 382.

resources for the annihilation of the British Empire". Lastly, he is reported to have said that he would see to it "that the British Government was prepared for the time when the Runciman mission might fail". In a covering letter to Weizsäcker, Theo Kordt added:

> Sir Horace spoke of the possibility of a special envoy of the British Government communicating to the Führer a proposal of a wide (*grosszügig*), peaceful solution; still, all effort in this direction would be useless if there was any truth in the rumours current in London and on the Continent of our having fixed a date for invading Czechoslovakia. I specially pointed out to Sir Horace how necessary it now was for the British Government to speak and act clearly. Beneš and his people should not be allowed to believe that the old policy of cheating could be continued because of British indecision.
>
> Following my instructions I did not mention a plebiscite in the Sudetenland as a possible solution. But from the whole course of the conversation, Wilson can have no doubt that we would not agree to a solution which left the [Czechoslovak] State intact within its present frontiers.

Thus Theo Kordt seems to have spoken in favour of breaking up Czechoslovakia before he was instructed to do so. And this is what, after Munich, he told his brother about his talk with Horace Wilson:

> I told him frankly that I and my friends thought Hitler to be driving to war; but he should tell Neville Chamberlain that the German people abhorred war, and that a steady policy on the part of the British Government could alone make him desist.

He further quoted Sir Horace as mentioning

> the possibility of a personal letter from Chamberlain to Hitler making clear the situation beyond all doubt. Sir Horace asked me to draft such a letter, appropriate, in the view of the German Opposition, to

open the eyes of the German people. Later the correspondence was to be published.

How much truth there is in either report Sir Horace Wilson alone could say. But the two versions are not incompatible: the Czechs were to be ground still further between the millstones of German blackmail and British "mediation", while the appeasers were to be asked to help the "good Germans" to stop Hitler from exposing Germany to mortal danger — as was done at Munich.

Early in September it was decided to ask the British Government for "an unambiguous declaration concerning their attitude should Hitler attack Czechoslovakia" — they should "show their teeth", for Hitler maintained that they were keeping "all their back-doors open in case their bluff did not come off". Erich Kordt could not go to London but a cousin of his went, having learnt by heart instructions he had written for her, and on September 6 Theo Kordt, in a two hours' talk, gave the message to Sir Horace Wilson. Asked if he would repeat it to Lord Halifax, he gladly agreed, and on September 7, met him in Wilson's room at 10 Downing Street. And here is the account given by Theo Kordt to his brother:

> I had previously jotted down what I wanted to say, and started: "Extraordinary times demand extraordinary means. To-day I come to you not as German Chargé d'Affaires, but as spokesman of political and military circles in Berlin, which desire by every means to prevent war. The message which I shall now transmit to you has been carefully considered and seems to us to deserve the British Government's attention. We know for certain that Hitler plans an attack against Czechoslovakia and assumes that it will be possible to localize the war, *i.e.* that France will not meet her obligations towards Czechoslovakia arising from the alliance of January 25, 1924, and the subsequent agreements connected with it. The political and military circles for which I

speak sharply oppose that policy. We believe that a return to decency and honour among European nations would be definitely barred if free rein was now given to Hitler's policy of violence.

"Lloyd George declared after the World War that the nations and governments had slipped into it. The men for whom I speak consider that the position in 1914 would not have proved so hopeless if Sir Edward Grey had made it clear on behalf of the Government that Great Britain would not stand aside in case of a Franco-German war. This warning given in time would have had a moderating influence on the decisions of the Imperial Government.

"If, therefore, France is willing to fulfil her obligations towards her Czechoslovak ally, and if the declarations of the Prime Minister that in such case the British Empire could not stand aside are meant seriously, my friends consider it necessary that the British Government should clearly emphasize these decisive facts. The declaration we suggest cannot be too unequivocal and firm enough for the purpose in question. Hitler and Ribbentrop will hardly dare to launch a war if a public British declaration brings it home to the German people that an attack against Czechoslovakia would render war with Great Britain inevitable. Should, however, Hitler persist in his bellicose policy, I can assure you that the political and military circles for which I speak will 'take arms against a sea of troubles and by opposing end them'.

"Hitler's war is unpopular with German public opinion and in responsible army circles, and is considered a crime against civilization. If the solicited declaration is issued, the leaders are prepared to offer armed resistance to Hitler's policy. A diplomatic defeat would result in a very serious political reverse for Hitler within Germany and would practically mean the end of the National-Socialist régime."

I concluded: "It was not easy for me to speak in this way to the British Foreign Secretary. But

> German patriots see no other way out of the dilemma except in close co-operation with the British Government in order to prevent the great crime of a war."
>
> Lord Halifax listened to me in a most earnest and attentive manner. He thanked me for the frankness with which I had spoken at this most critical moment. He, too, emphasized that war over the Sudeten problem would be a crime; but it would become inevitable if Hitler used force against Czechoslovakia. Halifax promised to inform the Prime Minister and one or two of his colleagues in the Cabinet, and assured me that the matter would be carefully examined and treated as secret.

Eloquent enough to impress the orator himself — but what was there of concrete data to make a responsible statesman take crucial decisions? A message from an alleged Fronde of undisclosed composition and unknown strength, whose capacity to act at the time remains uncertain even now. Halifax himself wrote to Henderson on August 5 that the Germans would hardly try to enforce their claims against Czechoslovakia if convinced "that it meant a general war". But how to convince them "without exposing ourselves to humiliation if we don't go to war"? — which the British Government had no intention of doing. Halifax's recipe was "to keep the Germans guessing". But Hitler had guessed, and guessed correctly; the other Germans had not; hence the trouble in their camp. When on September 15 Chamberlain's plane had taken off on his first flight to Germany, Halifax, according to Theo Kordt, took him by the arm and led him aside; and referring to the previous idea of a letter to Hitler, remarked: "We have in the meantime decided otherwise, and think a personal interview the better plan". No doubt Berchtesgaden, Godesberg, and Munich were the simplest and safest way of avoiding a war over Czechoslovakia. But the Germans themselves had not thought such a surrender possible.

Of Erich Kordt's contribution to the story of the alleged military plot against Hitler, in September 1938, the reader must form his own judgment. On the 27th, the day the German mobilization was expected at 2 P.M., his brother telephoned to him from London soon after 11 A.M. calling attention to the supreme gravity of the situation.

> I had hardly put down the receiver when I heard at the outer door of my office a knock agreed upon with Schulenburg [Deputy-Chief of the Berlin Police, executed after the attempt against Hitler of July 20, 1944]. He was no less excited than myself. " Brauchitsch is said to be willing to co-operate. I have come to ascertain whether the international situation is unchanged ", he said in haste. " The great war may start any moment ", I replied. " Immediate action is necessary before our plot is discovered. Don't wait till the afternoon or till to-morrow ", I begged him. He inquired who was in the Reich Chancellery. I could assure him that no precautions had yet been taken. . . . " I can get you into the Reich Chancellery. If several of us are inside, we may be able to open the great door behind the guard and let in an advance detachment into the Chancellery." Schulenburg hurried away. Now Rome was on the telephone.

The Italians were intervening in favour of a Four Power Conference at Munich. The crisis was over.

If the risks of Hitler's policy alone provoked active opposition, its moral basis was weak and its work necessarily uncertain. Erich Kordt admits perhaps more than he meant to when he says that the mass of the German people were ready

> to pass over doubts and pangs of conscience, which subsisted in spite of intensive propaganda, so long as no obvious risks or dangers were seen. The feeling for justice and the wish for peace lost their

> strength through the seeming ease with which Hitler entered Prague.

A " conscience " and " feeling for justice " born of fear and evaporated by success will raise no martyrs; and about the second " plot " against Hitler, in the autumn of 1939, Kordt writes under the heading: " Thus conscience does make cowards of us all ".

The German General Staff did not believe in an easy victory over France. General Beck, late C.G.S., declared that an offensive in the West " must get stuck "—

> where I cannot say, but my military experience of forty years tells me that it will get stuck. Then comes the historic counter-offensive.

Brauchitsch and Halder thought likewise.

> At last [writes Kordt] the General Staff seemed seriously engaged on preparing a *coup d'état*, to be carried out the moment Hitler gave the order for an autumn offensive in the West. . . . On secret instructions from Halder a staff was set up . . . to plan in detail military action against Hitler. . . . The plan began to take shape.

But were the generals ready to act? " If only they do not again plead the oath which, as they say, binds them to the living Hitler! " remarked Oster (Canaris's assistant — both executed by the Germans in April 1945).

With engaging frankness Kordt discusses why not one man was found among those who had easy access to Hitler " to free our country and the world from that man ". He himself " had better chances than anyone of our group "; but the idea of acting " I always dropped with suspicious speed ".

> There is no lack of brave men and women; . . . but few among them are prepared to strive for an end and renounce seeing it accomplished. All

watchfulness . . . can protect a tyrant only against those who mean to witness the sequel. . . .

" We have no one to throw a bomb so as to free our generals of their scruples ", said Oster when I called on him on November 1, 1939.

" I have come to ask you for it " . . .

" You shall have it on November 11 ", he replied. . . .

Then, on the 8th, occurred the attempt against Hitler in the Munich beer-cellar — Oster suspected that it had been staged by the Gestapo with Hitler's knowledge.

" And now ? " I asked impatiently.

" Watch them [replied Oster] ; now our swaying reeds will say : the dirty work is being taken from us, Hitler will fall without us."

" Then we have to proceed without them. The decision stands. Well, see you to-morrow."

But the next day Oster explained that, for technical reasons, it was impossible after the attempt to do anything without rousing suspicion.

Then I said quietly : " In that case I must use a pistol, the offensive in the West *must not* be ".

Oster argued against it — the offensive had been postponed by a fortnight.

I have not used a pistol.

" It is all over ", I said at night to my cousin, and begged her to ask no questions.

And Kordt concludes :

It was neither an accident, nor fate, but our insufficiency which has got us where we now stand.

A fitting end to a tale which, even accepting the " historicity " of the curiously melodramatic conversations, might as well, from the point of view of history, have been left untold.

A diplomatic counterpart to " conspiratorial " activities was sought by the Kordt brothers in private interviews with Lord Vansittart, mostly at the house of Mr. Conwell-Evans; and whatever Vansittart may have thought of them, he could hardly have refused meeting the Counsellor or Chargé d'Affaires of the German Embassy and the *chef de cabinet* of Ribbentrop. Accounts of those talks are prefaced by Erich Kordt with descriptions of Vansittart's person and of his checked trousers, remarks which Conwell-Evans's housekeeper made about Vansittart and Theo Kordt, etc.; the talks as rendered equal these preliminaries in taste and importance. The Kordts are seen instructing Vansittart and H.M. Government in the conduct of foreign affairs: criticizing the guarantees given to secondary Powers in Eastern Europe; advising how to deal with Italy; or warning the British Government on behalf of the German " Opposition " to close with Stalin lest Hitler forestall them — their guidance was apparently required to put Englishmen wise and to set things right. At the last interview between Theo Kordt and Vansittart, on the eve of the outbreak of war, it was " settled " that Kordt should try to be sent to a neutral country so as to keep in touch with London: and Weizsäcker, in fact, agreed to place him at Berne to deal with Switzerland (the " Protecting Power ") and with the Red Cross. And here is the method of communicating which Theo Kordt claims to have been arranged:

> I was to address a postcard to Vansittart, Conwell-Evans, or to Vansittart's secretary . . . unsigned, only with a verse of Horace. A fortnight after despatching the postcard I would be available at the place of the postmark. Lord Vansittart would then send Conwell-Evans to meet me.

Both Weizsäcker and Erich Kordt emphasize how careful they had to be in dealings even with trusted foreign diplomatists because of the dangers arising from stolen documents and broken ciphers. Kordt writes in his book (page 251):

> Ciano had supplied us with evidence that even the archives of the British Foreign Office did not guard all their secrets.

And at Weizsäcker's trial he said in the witness-box, on June 4, 1948 (page 7370):

> We had heard from the Austrians that Mussolini presented to Schuschnigg whole files . . . evidently . . . stolen from the Foreign Office archives.

Had Erich Kordt, in June 1948, to rely on such third-hand, inaccurate information about that matter? Had brother Theo said nothing to brother Erich? And had not Erich heard or read Theo's Nuremberg evidence before he wrote his memoirs published in 1950? Why, then, so discreet or reticent? Of course, to a hundred readers of memoirs there will be hardly one who will wade through the mass of the Nuremberg records. Here are the replies Theo Kordt gave on July 15, 1948, under cross-examination by the American prosecuting counsel:

> *Q*. . . . during that period [in Switzerland] . . . you were also in contact with the British intermediaries in your peace and resistance efforts, isn't that correct?
>
> *A*. Yes.
>
> *Q*. At that time . . . you certainly were doing nothing to harm British interests, were you? . . .
>
> *A*. Nothing that would be contrary to my official duties and my personal convictions.
>
> *Q*. Now, do you recall that in December 1939 you were the person selected to go to Italy?
>
> *A*. Yes.
>
> *Q*. . . . for the examination of black-market documents of the British Foreign Office and its missions in Italy? . . .
>
> *A*. I know what you are referring to.

Theo Kordt further stated (correctly) that the documents were not from the Foreign Office archives but from the Rome Embassy; (incorrectly) that they were only drafts; and (confusedly) that he was sent to ascertain their authenticity because he " knew the handwriting of leading officials in the British Foreign Office ".

> *Q.* Were there just a few documents or more . . . ?
> *A.* . . . There were two hand suitcases full.

He had looked at them twice, each time for only about twenty minutes; obviously had not been able to examine them carefully; yet he knew that they were " amusing " but unimportant; and had recommended their purchase — for their historical value. Pressed about the use to which copies of cipher telegrams among them could be put in breaking British codes, Kordt wriggled till shown a wire which he himself had sent to Weizsäcker naming this as a reason for purchasing them. " Well," he then remarked, " all countries make that effort. . . ."

> *Q.* Now, subsequently you saw . . . your British friends. Did you discuss with them the fact that these documents were now in German hands?
> *A.* No.

Questioned about other activities detrimental to Great Britain (transmitting via Berne information from the German Legation at Dublin about air targets in Britain, etc.) Theo Kordt asserted that he did nothing beyond " what a diplomat of every country has to do for his own country ". This may be true — except that the Kordts should not at the same time have claimed the confidence of Englishmen, nor should try now to represent their own and Weizsäcker's war activities as something which they were not: the primary aim for which they worked was Germany's victory, and next, reinsurance in case of defeat.

When in October 1939 plans for a military *coup* against Hitler were talked about, Erich Kordt, together with

Hasso von Etzdorf, the official *liaison* between the General Staff and the Foreign Ministry, drew up a memorandum discussing, among other things, the conditions for a peace with the Western Powers. The memorandum was submitted to the C.-in-C., Brauchitsch, to the General Staff, to General von Stülpnagel and other Army leaders, and is said to have received their approval. Parts of it are now printed by Kordt; and here are its territorial terms for a " peace with honour ":

> . . . a peace which would not infringe Germany's ethnic frontier (approximately as fixed at Munich), and would establish an overland connexion between East Prussia and the Reich, and restore to Germany the Upper Silesian industrial districts.
>
> Such a solution would satisfy her real national interest. It would avoid burdening Germany with alien elements, and yet, for geographic and economic reasons, would secure for her a predominant influence over a rump-Czechia and a rump-Poland.

Thus the Munich frontier, which included some 800,000 Czechs in Germany, was claimed as just, while part or the whole of the Polish Corridor and of Upper Silesia was claimed without reference to " ethnology "; and it was fully and pleasurably realized that such a territorial settlement would give Germany the whip hand over the " rumps " of those two nations. The " good Germans " visibly change into Hitler profiteers.

Meantime it seemed essential to obtain from Great Britain an assurance that the confusion of a military *coup* would not be used for hostile action by the Allies. And lo! in the last days of October, Mrs. Theo Kordt arrived in Berlin with a written declaration brought to Berne by Conwell-Evans.

> Asked by my brother [writes Erich Kordt], Conwell-Evans assured him that this declaration by Neville Chamberlain, which was for transmission to him

> (*diese zur Übergabe an ihn bestimmte Erklärung Neville Chamberlains*) constituted a solemn obligation, strictly to be observed toward any trustworthy Government which would replace the Nazi régime.
>
> My brother and I had during the preceding days corresponded in code about the expected British declaration and referred to it as a " certificate of discharge " (*löschbare Quittung*), which I absolutely required in case we sold our parental house. " I am sending you enclosed the certificate of discharge ", he now wrote in his covering letter, " and I expect a sale soon."
>
> I was convinced that I now had a powerful trump in my hand with which to overcome the inhibitions of the General Staff.

" Oster has told me what you are bringing from the Tommies ", said General Beck, " now we must go ahead." Beck was greatly impressed.

So will be the reader, though for different reasons. A photographic copy of the document is given by Erich Kordt, and at the first glance the reader will note that this historic declaration, sent presumably by the Prime Minister himself, is scribbled very roughly by Mr. Conwell-Evans using informal abbreviations of his own (for instance, a short dash for " the ") ; next, that Erich Kordt, who prints it in English on the opposite page, substitutes " NC " for " HMG ", and makes no less than seven other mistakes in transcribing some 25 lines ; and lastly, that at the top of the photographic copy is the mark " Oct. 12 ", apparently added later, and neither reproduced nor explained on the opposite page. Turning to the document itself, he will be struck by its oratorical and homiletic emptiness : it wishes for a better future in which Germany will take her rightful place in Europe and all nations will be able " to live their lives without fear and to devote their gifts to the development of their culture, the pursuit of their ideals and the improvement of their national prosperity". But on comparing this declaration, "to be transmitted" to Theo Kordt, with *Hansard* for October 12, 1939, columns 565-6, the reader will find that it consisted of two paragraphs of Neville Chamberlain's speech, broadcast the same night to all the world. Surely the Berlin Foreign Office, the German Legation at Berne, and at least some of the generals must have been acquainted with it, and apparently the mark of "Oct. 12" is a reference to its origin. Why, then, has Erich Kordt nothing to say about that?

The final touch of comedy is added by the covering letter from Theo Kordt. If the two brothers had a secret code, why use it in connexion with a text which, however unimportant, would have supplied the Gestapo with the key?

General Guderian, the distinguished Armoured Corps commander, writes in his memoirs: "Much is now talked and written about resistance to the Hitler regime. . . . But I must refuse the description of resisters to men who merely whispered in corners that they were of a different opinion. . . ." He might have added: "and who expected the British Government to do their work for them".

PAUL SCHMIDT

Diplomacy by conference has produced a new art and profession: that of an interpreter capable of translating forthwith a long and weighty statement even to the satisfaction of a speaker who can follow the translation. For that more than a rich and ready vocabulary is required — to get the meaning of delicate shades and connotations in controversy the interpreter must have a good grasp of the subject; moreover, he must be alert, supremely attentive, impersonal, and discreet, and must have an equable temper and an excellent memory. Schmidt's book [1] bears the sub-heading: "Experiences of the Chief Interpreter in the Foreign Office with the Statesmen of Europe": during his twenty-two years with Stresemann and Brüning, Hitler, Göring, and Ribbentrop, he watched and heard and interpreted for practically all the leading men of the period. His position was well-nigh unique: he was sole witness of many of the most crucial *tête-à-tête* talks, and the minutes which he drew up are often their only, or at least their fullest, record: these minutes sometimes appear even in non-German collections of documents.

Dr. Schmidt might therefore be expected to have a momentous story to tell; but he has not. Opportunities have their inherent antidotes and limitations. The instincts and faculties of an incisive critical observer would hardly accord with the duties of a spiritually mute interpreter: a day-to-day diary or the original notes of

[1] *Statist auf diplomatischer Bühne, 1923–45,* by Dr. Paul Schmidt. Bonn: Athenäum Verlag.

secret talks would make first-rate historical material, but it would probably have been improper for Schmidt to have kept either. Friendly, good-natured, with a faint and unobtrusive sense of humour, but on the whole uncritical, he bore with all (Ribbentrop alone was too much for him): and his story reflects his personality. Now Stresemann is his hero — if only generous concessions had been promptly made to him! (the illegal rearmament of Weimar Germany and its purpose lie conveniently beyond Schmidt's purview); and, next, the Western Powers are blamed for having given in too much to Hitler — a justified charge, but unbecoming in those who willingly served him.

> Post-war discussion of events with which I had been so closely connected having shown me what incomplete or even misleading impressions are transmitted by sober documents, I decided to put down my reminiscences of almost a quarter of a century of European history.

These were to " combine the indispensable human element with the purely factual material ", and to keep to events of which he had been witness. But next he tries to supplement his own reminiscences and " notes " (*Aufzeichnungen* — their exact nature is not stated) by studying the works and memoirs of leading statesmen, and contemporary records.

> I went through the files of German newspapers and through the volumes of *The Times* and the *Temps* from 1923 to 1945, and many a detail of days gone by re-emerged before my eyes.

But while Schmidt would have done well had he properly checked his reminiscences, by padding them with extraneous matter he imperceptibly changed from a writer of memoirs into an historian — without the historian's equipment or outlook. Dry bones are clothed with flesh and sinews by one unversed in anatomy: often with comic results.

I take my examples from the years 1937 to 1939 with which I am best acquainted. Their treatment is meagre; the average space to a year is forty pages, as against twenty-one during the preceding fourteen years; and a good deal is filled with trifles. Of two important talks noted in 1937 the first is between Göring and Mussolini. On Sunday, April 25, Schmidt was suddenly summoned to Rome. Next day "in the afternoon I entered for the first time the famous Palazzo Venezia . . .". But there is in the *Ciano Diplomatic Papers* a long minute by Schmidt of a talk at the Palazzo Venezia on January 23, 1937; of the previous talk on January 15 I have seen none, though a good deal is known about it, at second hand, from diplomatic dispatches.[1] The account in Schmidt's memoirs of that on April 26 curiously resembles the talk of January 15: an unlikely repetition. Confusion and telescoping seem to render his new account unfit for historical consumption.

The second report is of Lord Halifax's talk with Hitler at Berchtesgaden on November 19. It is at variance with the official minute prepared by Schmidt himself. There Hitler hopes that the Agreement with Austria of July 11, 1936, would remove all difficulties; in Schmidt's memoirs Hitler insists on the "close connection between Austria and the Reich", urgently desired by the Austrian people "ever since 1919"—that is, the *Anschluss*. We are told by Schmidt (and could have guessed) that Hitler and Ribbentrop often doctored his minutes even for the German archives, and still more if communicated to the other side. But had Hitler insisted on the *Anschluss* he would hardly have gone back on it, especially in view of Halifax's mild reaction.

Under 1938 there is the minute of a talk between

[1] See below, page 122.

Henderson and Ribbentrop on May 21 — that is, of the British *démarche* at the time of the Czech mobilization. The reader would assume that for its lively exchanges Schmidt drew on his own memory or notes: but the selection and wording follow too closely Henderson's account in his *Failure of a Mission.* Next Schmidt turns critical historian:

> To-day we know from his [Henderson's] memoirs that the British Military Attaché and his assistant had reported after an extensive exploratory tour through Saxony and Silesia that they had seen no signs of unusual troop movements. . . . Why then he should have intervened with such energy is not quite clear to me even now.

Henderson states that the officers were sent out on May 21 [1] — even so the report of a tour of 500 to 700 miles could not have reached him the same day. But in fact they did not set out till May 22.[2]

Of Chamberlain's talk with Hitler at Berchtesgaden on September 15, 1938, Schmidt was the only witness, and his minute is published in the captured German documents, while a slightly doctored version supplied by the Germans and a note by Chamberlain appear in the British documents. To these Schmidt now adds some "human" touches. Hitler having expressed his determination to settle the Czech problem "in one way or another", Chamberlain asked excitedly why then had Hitler let him come to Germany — there was no sense in it, and he had better leave immediately.

> Hitler hesitated for a moment. . . . I looked at him with tense expectation. In that second "war

[1] Page 135.

[2] See *Documents on British Foreign Policy, 1919–1939,* Third Series, vol. i, page 344; Henderson's wire of May 22, 1938 (no. 268): "When I told Herr von Weizsäcker last night that my two Military Attachés were motoring today towards the Czechoslovakian frontier to see for themselves . . ."

> and peace " were finely balanced. But the amazing thing happened. Hitler drew back.

If, he said, Chamberlain was prepared to apply the principle of self-determination to the Sudetens he was ready to discuss its application.

Here then is a dramatic scene to enrich historical narratives. But in Schmidt's own minute almost half a page of argument intervenes between Chamberlain's question and Hitler's alleged reply; and with ten pages covering three hours, the seconds of tense silence change into five to ten minutes' lively conversation. Also in Chamberlain's own minute there is talking to and fro between question and " reply ".

Taken as a whole, Schmidt's book is much too long for light reading — nearly six hundred large pages — with too little entertainment to the square yard; while for a source-book it is too inaccurate, or at least too unreliable.

PART II

SURRENDER TO DANGER

PROLEGOMENA TO THE "ANSCHLUSS"

At the end of the First World War it was left to the Germans to produce their own story of their pre-war diplomacy in a vast collection of documents, *Die Grosse Politik*, finely tempered to extenuate Germany's war guilt. At the close of the Second, the Allies were determined to obtain the full record of Germany's foreign policy, and the advancing armies were instructed to keep watch for enemy archives, with experts in readiness to examine them. For mass and contents the haul from secret storage places has exceeded expectations: Nazi orders to destroy the most important portions had been carried out very incompletely, and were difficult to execute with regard to documents in multiple copies; Germans, eager to curry favour, handed over archives of which they were custodians; and in the documents their authors, meticulous and unsqueamish, were often found to have recorded their malfeasance with disarming frankness. The British and American Governments, subsequently joined by the French, agreed to publish a selection from those archives in order to "establish a record of German foreign policy preceding and during World War II", and foremost historians in the three countries were entrusted with the work: left full freedom and merely enjoined to aim at "the highest scholarly objectivity", they took as fundamental test in selecting documents for publication their value "for an understanding of German foreign policy". The task was colossal: here were archives, in a disordered and incomplete condition, first dispersed in 1943 because of air-raids from the west, and a year later shifted again because of the rapid Russian advance from the east — " tens of thousands of bundles . . . repeatedly packed, moved by train, truck, or plane, and then unpacked and shelved ", hurriedly, under war conditions. Important files, first listed as missing, have since been found not to be missing after all; and not until this gigantic jig-saw puzzle is completed will it be possible to say definitely what has, or has not, survived.

> The order in which documents should be presented in a collection such as this has long been a disputed subject among historians. The editors have agreed that documents should be grouped by topics; within each topic they are presented in the chronological order in which they originated.

" In this age of shorthand and the typewriter, documents grow in number and length " — which renders unitary chronological publication increasingly difficult. On the other hand, arrangement by " topics " is apt to dissever cognate matter: in this series it has separated Austria and Czechoslovakia, which in 1938 presented closely interconnected problems. Moreover, various topics open at different dates, and of the chapters dealing with the six themes which are covered by this volume,[1] that on relations between Germany and Austria starts with the Agreement of July 11, 1936, on which they hinged during the immediate pre-*Anschluss* period, while the other five chapters are made to begin at various dates between March and November 1937: the dates on the title-page, " September, 1937–September, 1938 ", are therefore a mere approximation to a chronologically jagged tale. March 7, 1936, the crucial date of the remilitarization of the Rhineland, might have offered a better starting-point for a unitary presentation up to Munich at least, of Germany's relations with Austria, Czechoslovakia, and

[1] *Documents on German Foreign Policy, 1918–1945*, Series D (1937–1945) vol. i, *From Neurath to Ribbentrop* (*September 1937–September 1938*).

Poland, and with the Great Powers of Western Europe in so far as they converged on these problems.

Even to the Agreement of July 11, 1936, March 7 supplies the background. Abyssinia broke up the Stresa front; the Rhineland crisis exposed the political and moral weakness of the Western Powers; the victory of the Popular Front in France and of the Reds in Spain increased ideological tensions in the Mediterranean; Austria could no longer count on effective foreign support in maintaining her independence. An idea, canvassed by Franz von Papen, German Ambassador in Vienna, was now taken up, and *Operation Franz* resulted in the Agreement of July 11, which professed to aim at a resumption " of normal and friendly relations " between Germany and Austria. The German Government recognized Austria's full sovereignty, while she acknowledged herself a German State whose policy in general, " and particularly with regard to the German Reich", should be based on that principle. Although National-Socialism within Austria was declared her " internal affair ", the Austrian Government promised Germany to grant " a far-reaching amnesty " to the Austrian Nazis, help to solve the problem of Austrian Nazi refugees in Germany, and admit the so-called " National Opposition " to a share in political life. Cultural and Press relations between Germany and Austria were to be promoted, and associations of each other's nationals were to be allowed provided they did not interfere in the internal political affairs of the host country. In short, it was agreed to pretend that Austria's independence would not suffer through her being taken in tow, or from Nazi activities within her borders. On that impracticable document, superscribed " Gentlemen's Agreement ", the relations between the two Governments were made to turn for the next year and a half, a period of uneasy compromises and subterfuges, of tribulations and sudden reversals on the Austrian side, and of pressure from Germany exerted in a fitful and incoherent manner.

The *Anschluss*, first attempted by Hitler in July 1934, retained top place in his foreign program; whereas with Schuschnigg " the maintenance of complete Austrian independence was an article of faith ". The Nazis claimed that a " National-minded " majority of Austrians was prevented by an " insignificant minority " in office from declaring its " joyous adherence to the Reich ". In fact, both were minorities, with the Socialists opposed to either; the semi-Fascist régime, set up by Dollfuss and maintained in a milder form by Schuschnigg, rested on a narrow basis; none the less a Nazi revolution could not have succeeded, and Hitler saw that the " solution " had therefore to " emanate from Germany " — yet he fluctuated between " evolutionary means " and a resort to force. While watching and testing the international balance of forces, he tried by Nazi infiltrations to corrode the Austrian régime from within, and thus to reach " an automatic solution ". Schuschnigg, on the other hand, mixed compliance with obstruction: without a feasible plan or the means for effective self-defence, he dallied in truly Austrian fashion, hoping for a miracle or the chapter of accidents to rescue Austria from her parlous situation. Thus both he and Hitler were awaiting events and awkwardly manœuvring, hampered rather than aided by their following whose spirits and cohesion they had to sustain: Schuschnigg, while trying to placate Hitler, had to reassure the Fatherland Front by pronouncements compromising towards Hitler; and Hitler, while feeding the Nazi ferment in Austria, had to guard against being forced by its ebullitions to act at an inconvenient moment. Meantime Papen, an easy-going intriguer, preached to the Austrian Nazis that " the ultimate decision " lay outside Austria, that the Party could play only " a passive rôle", and that its first duty was "not to disturb the European policy of the Führer". According to him the aim of the Agreement was to "exclude Austria from international discussion", to wreck attempts at a Habsburg restoration, and by "German spiritual penetration" effectively to check the growth of "an indigenous Austrian culture".

On the day the Agreement was signed, the German Ambassador, von Hassell, told Mussolini that the Germans "were still concerned about the Habsburg agitation". In Berlin, the Austrian Minister asked a Wilhelmstrasse official if the Agreement would really be carried out by the Party authorities, and was told that this would undoubtedly be done honestly; a month later, a high German official inquired of a leading terrorist refugee of 1934, "what demands . . . should be made of the Austrian Government for the further implementation of the Agreement"; while Goebbels is known secretly to have told the German Press that the fight against Austria continued, and Hitler to have received representatives of the Austrian Nazis. But as Papen reported in one of his long and muddled dispatches, "for lack of a strict Party leadership" many Austrian Nazis did not yet know what course to adopt.

On July 23 an amnesty was published by Vienna covering more than 15,000 Nazis; only some 150 terrorists, including men concerned in the murder of Dollfuss, remained in prison; and even these, the subject of bitter German complaints, were gradually being released; while "Hitler vacations" for released Nazi prisoners from Austria were arranged in Germany by the Labour Front. More difficult was the problem of the Nazi refugees; they numbered about 40,000, and admittedly their early mass return was not desired: intercepted letters showed them hostile to the Austrian State and threatening "further acts of violence". Many had adopted German nationality, and had received military training in the S.S. or the Nazi Austrian Legion; and that Legion was continued even after July 11, with cadres and muster-roll ready for mobilization. In the end hardly any of the refugees were repatriated under the July Agreement.

To attempt "real pacification" in Austria by unfettering Nazi activities was a contradiction which henceforth coloured every relevant declaration or measure. In the July Agreement Schuschnigg declared himself prepared to work out with representatives of the so-called "National Opposition" a plan for its participation "in the shaping of the political will in Austria"; but he reserved to himself the choice of the "appropriate moment" and of the representatives: concrete promises were rendered indefinite by reservations concerning time and persons. Early in November, Glaise von Horstenau, a Nazi agent, was made Minister of the Interior, another Nazi fellow-traveller Director of Security, while Ministers particularly obnoxious to the Nazis were dropped. This, Schuschnigg told Papen, was public testimony to his resolve to stand by the July 11 policy; but he added that regard for the Fatherland Front compelled him to move slowly. The National Opposition, encouraged by the two Nazi Ministers, now asked to be allowed openly to form an organization which would enable them "to exercise a legal influence on political events in Austria". While combating "the Austrian ideology", they demanded political equality with the Government party in a totalitarian, single-party State; which Nazi advance might well have sufficed to demoralize and break up the Fatherland Front. In February 1937, Schuschnigg entered into direct negotiations with the Austrian Nazis; assured them of his desire to maintain contact with them and to help them "to establish liaison in national matters" with the Fatherland Front; and promised to facilitate their activities, but begged them not to press for formal recognition. "The program of pacification", Glaise said in April 1937 to the German Chargé d'Affaires,

> will consist in the long-drawn-out bungling that is typical of Austria until such time as conditions are ripe for the final, natural solution of German-Austrian relations.

Meantime wearisome negotiations were proceeding between the two Governments concerning the rights of Reich Germans in Austria: were they to be free to give the Hitler salute, to wear Nazi badges, or to hoist the Nazi flag? Was the display of *Mein Kampf* in shop windows, and were news-reels showing Hitler, to be permitted? "Mutuality" in such matters was meaningless; Austria had nothing to propagate in Germany; but to affirm the Nazi creed in Austria was to demonstrate against her separate existence. Still, to prohibit such displays was, according to Papen, a policy of "rude rebuffs to the interests and the symbols of the Reich", resulting in a situation of "extraordinary gravity". "It would require only another incident", he told Schuschnigg on May 26, 1937, "to touch off an explosion the consequences of which no one could foresee."

German official reports on the Nazi Party in Austria were hardly favourable: the old Nazi leaders, freed by the amnesty, were squabbling with the younger men; the leader of the "illegal Party", Captain Leopold, a typical former Austrian N.C.O., was said to be "removing all clever and intelligent people . . . from influential posts"; and he engaged in a vigorous personal and policy feud with various Party offices in the Reich — of which, wrote Papen, too many were "concerning themselves with Austrian policy". Yet administrative chaos in Germany and violent quarrels within the Austrian Nazi Party rendered only more difficult Schuschnigg's task of placating his opponents. Papen assured him that Hitler would have the Austrian Nazis choose their own political line;

and he urged Berlin not to let it appear that these were shaping their policy in accordance with instructions received from the Reich. But the Austrian Government had in fact evidence on the point which it did not dare to produce: early in May 1937 they were reported to have seized memoranda of conversations of Austrian Nazis with Hitler, proofs that funds and propaganda material were being supplied from Germany, etc.; and in a raid of the Vienna Nazi headquarters in the Teinfaltstrasse, on January 25, 1938, they found a "Program for Action for the Year 1938" which argued that nothing could be expected from Schuschnigg and that a German invasion was the only solution, to be followed by the setting up of a Nazi Government, and a plebiscite. Even this discovery the Austrian Government could not turn to account: it would have infuriated Hitler without securing effective foreign support. In fact, the raid in the Teinfaltstrasse, according to Papen, merely made Schuschnigg "conscious of the impossibility of letting the present state of affairs continue" and "eager for a personal meeting" with Hitler: it prodded him to undertake the ill-fated journey to Berchtesgaden on February 12, 1938.

There had been numerous meetings between German and Austrian statesmen during the seventeen months July 1936–February 1938 (more even than recorded in the captured documents). In October 1936, Göring, always debonair and braggart, breezily told Schuschnigg that if Germany desired the *Anschluss* this would be merely the concern of "the nearest German divisional commander", for the Italians would not intervene; but he preferred to talk of a *Zusammenschluss* ("convergence"): for instance, a common currency and tariff. In November, Guido Schmidt, Austrian Foreign Minister since July 11, visited Berlin; clever and ambitious, he wanted to make "contacts with Reich personalities". The protocol to be signed was settled beforehand: a joint declaration against Communism and a mutual promise not to join without previous consulation any new economic *bloc* in the Danube basin (the Czechoslovak Prime Minister, Hodža, was planning one) were followed by Austrian concessions, mainly " in the cultural field ". On November 19 Schmidt was received by Hitler, and after a short (unrecorded) private talk, which seems to have greatly impressed Schmidt, he was treated to an extensive *tour d'horizon*: Hitler discoursed on the Communist danger; thought it acute in France; inveighed against the French and Czech pacts with Soviet Russia; spoke favourably of Rumania and Yugoslavia as " outposts against Bolshevism " — Hungary should direct her revisionist claims against one quarter only [Czechoslovakia]. Consolidation should start through a federation of Germany, Italy, Austria, and Hungary; to be joined by Spain, perhaps by Poland, or even France; by Rumania and Yugoslavia. He said some friendly words about the British, whose mentality is sober " and can be influenced only by force ".

> I experienced this myself when I conferred with Sir Simon [*sic*] here in Berlin. Only when I assured him that the German Air Force had reached the strength of that of the English were we able to express ourselves with mutual respect; thus our naval agreement came into being.

Neurath, in a concluding talk on November 21, tried to impress Schmidt (who showed fear of the " dynamism " of the Nazi movement, and " of the huge German State ") with the need of further and more speedy concessions to " the National forces in Austria ", and of " discontinuing the repressive measures " against them. Still, a circular, issued the same day, to the German diplomatic missions abroad described Schmidt's visit as " satisfactory in every respect "; while according to Papen " deep inner satisfaction " was felt in Vienna: the great success of the trip had " eased the psychological tension ".

Then followed a characteristic *contretemps*. On the 26th, Schuschnigg, addressing officials of the Fatherland Front, said that the Agreement of July 11 did not affect Austrian domestic policy, and that the Fatherland movement had three opponents: Communism, Nazism, and defeatism in its own ranks — Nazism within Austria being " an enemy ". When taken to task by the Germans, he explained that his remarks had been extemporaneous and intended for a small circle only of party officials who had to be reassured; and when told by Papen that the July Agreement must not be made into a façade behind which to continue " a particularistic Austrian policy ", Schuschnigg replied that " he fully recognized Austria's historical mission within the framework of the new German Reich ", under Berlin leadership. On a later occasion he assured Papen of his determination

> to place the political and moral forces of Austria at the disposal of the German nation in the struggle to regain its world position. . . . Since the Führer himself had declared that the historical differences with France had been settled, the future of the Reich could lie only in south-eastern Europe. Austria was predestined for this mission by history and by natural capacity. She should therefore be permitted to retain the character she had formed in the course of a millennium and not be yoked to any sort of centralized system directed from Berlin.

Further, being a Catholic country, she should not be drawn into certain " ideological controversies ".

> If both conditions could be met it would not be impossible to find a constitutional formula that would enable Austria to cooperate closely with the Reich.

Here then was the old Austrian song, repeated with variants for a century past; now a song *d'outre-tombe*.

The ill-humour evoked in Berlin by Schuschnigg's address of November 26 found expression on the 28th in a second diplomatic circular about Schmidt's visit, professing to be a continuation of the previous one: Schmidt had raised "the Habsburg question", and was told of the "dire consequences" which an attempted restoration would have for Austria; at the request of the Czechs, he had inquired whether the Germans "were prepared to inaugurate an improvement in German-Czech relations"; and it was concluded from his talk that the Austrian Government meant "to rely heavily on Italy for support", and did not "seem averse to entering into closer political and economic relations with Czechoslovakia" (than which hardly anything more ominous could have been said about them by the Germans).

In January 1937, Göring, on a visit to Rome, told Hassell

> that he would take up the Austrian question with Mussolini. . . . Italy should keep hands off Austria and recognize her as a German sphere of interest so that even an *Anschluss* could be carried out if we so desired. . . . He feared that in view of the domestic policy of the Austrian Government another crisis would soon occur there, and provision would have to be made to prevent such events from again affecting German-Italian relations. . . .

Hassell replied that the Duce was "convinced of the inevitability of a gradual union of the two German States", but feared the *Anschluss* because of the Brenner frontier and of possible further German expansion to the south-east; and therefore Hassell advised Göring to emphasize that the question was not acute, and that no change would be made in the status of Austria without consulting Rome. On January 15 Göring apparently told Mussolini that the *Anschluss* was bound to come; but this being ill received, in the next talk, on the 23rd, he tried to "present the matter in a somewhat different light ".[1] Mussolini replied that he did not mean to resume "the Watch on the Brenner "; but that the German-Austrian Agreement of July 11, " an important pillar of German-Italian understanding and cooperation ", was binding on both parties; and that he would press the Austrian Government to carry it out faithfully. Göring in Rome complained to all and sundry of the " persecutions " of Nazis in Austria; of Russian troops and munitions for Spain passing through Austria; of a Habsburg restoration " being continually discussed "; and he discoursed on the " exceedingly serious view " which Germany took of the situation.

During Neurath's visit to Vienna in February 1937 (Nazi demonstrations greeted his coming, and counter-demonstrations by the Fatherland Front accompanied his departure), he declared both to Schmidt and Schuschnigg that a Habsburg restoration in Austria would not be tolerated by Germany; and when told that " the form of government was exclusively a matter for the Austrian State ", retorted that the Germans " had a very great interest in the state of domestic affairs in Austria ", and that such a restoration " would be the surest way for Austria to commit suicide ".

> The Reich [he said] would never sanction a historical development which, like the separation of the Netherlands and Switzerland from the German body politic, would necessarily result in a further weakening of the German nation in Europe.

In Rome on May 3, Neurath renewed to Mussolini Göring's assurances that Germany " did not intend any

[1] There is no printed minute of the conversation of January 15; a minute by Schmidt of that of the 23rd is in the *Ciano Papers*. Moreover there is second-hand information about both meetings: in Hassell's reports of what Göring and Ciano had told him; in reports from the Austrian Minister in Rome (see *Der Hochverratsprozess gegen Dr. Guido Schmidt*, pages 515-16); and in the account of those conversations given by Mussolini to Schuschnigg in Venice, on April 22, 1937 (see minute in the *Ciano Papers*).

surprises or rash actions " with regard to Austria, but declared once more that she " would not tolerate a Habsburg restoration ". When on June 24, 1937, a new strategic plan was issued for the German Armed Forces, special provision was made for " armed intervention against Austria in case of a monarchical restoration ".

Neurath again met Schmidt in Vorarlberg on August 8; called the Schuschnigg Government unrepresentative of the Austrian people; talked sharply about the treatment of the Austrian exiles, and urged Schmidt to resume discussions for a Customs union. The impression which Neurath professed to have carried away from the interview was that there was not the will in Austria to carry out the Agreement of July 11, 1936, " and that we shall hardly succeed in regulating German-Austrian relations by this method "; while Papen reported that Schmidt " appeared to be very well satisfied " with the conversation: " you . . . had, as usual, been very pleasant ". But (perhaps taking his cue from Neurath) Papen now struck a new note: Schuschnigg finds it difficult to stand up to the Fatherland Front, and Schmidt has lost his influence on Schuschnigg — he has become a mere pawn, unable " to put through his own program ". And on September 1: " With a continuation of the Schuschnigg methods we shall *very soon* be in an untenable position "; it may be necessary to consider " bringing about a change of Chancellor ". On September 25 Mussolini was due in Germany, and it was decided to bring up the question of Austria in order

> to secure Italian non-interference in plans for a gradual economic and military *rapprochement* with Austria. The façade of Austrian independence is to be maintained in view of Mussolini's repeated statements on this question.

Little is known about what was actually said, except that on September 27 Hitler gave Göring:

> the necessary instructions for his conversations with Mussolini regarding Austria. The Führer did not approve of Göring's previous policy, which was too severe, and stated that Germany should cause no explosion of the Austrian problem in the foreseeable future, but that we should continue to seek an evolutionary solution.

Only should the question be " exploded by another party ", Germany wanted freedom to intervene. In these talks Mussolini clearly showed his disapproval of Schuschnigg (to whom he had been grossly discourteous during the visit in Venice).

Hitler was free to twist and turn, rush forward or hang back, accountable to no one; but at certain junctures he would enunciate his foreign policy to his closest collaborators. Thus at the conference of November 5, 1937 (minuted in the " Hossbach notes "), he developed to them his ideas on how to solve the crucial problem of " living space" for the German people. Force would be necessary to achieve expansion, and it was " his unalterable resolve " to settle the problem at the latest by 1943–1945, or earlier should France be paralysed by internal strife or by war with another State. The annexation of Austria and Czechoslovakia would then be his first objective; it would strengthen Germany's economic position and remove the threat to her flank " in any possible operation against the West ". A paralysis of will in France without civil or foreign war was adumbrated, but probably had not yet hardened even in Hitler's thoughts into a third opening for action. He expressed the belief " that almost certainly Britain, and probably France as well, had already tacitly written off the Czechs ", and that they would not go to war over Austria or Czechoslovakia. And when told by Generals Blomberg and Fritsch that France, even at war with Italy, would retain a marked military superiority over Germany, whose western fortifications were as yet of small value and whose motorized divisions were "still more or less incapable of movement", Hitler repeated "that he was convinced of Britain's non-participation, and therefore did not believe in the probability of belligerent action by France against Germany".

Here, then, starts the fateful chain of events. Hitler was resolved on war, but basically expected it only in about five years' time; his generals were convinced that Germany would nowise be ready at an earlier date; even some foreign Powers knew of that time-table (for instance, the Poles, whom it helped to miscalculate their own long-term preparations); Mussolini still harped on it even in August 1939. But perhaps the Western Powers would not fight after all — in which case there was no need to wait or dally; and their behaviour in March 1936 suggested that this might be so. And now, at the critical juncture, the Western appeasers became active, as if intent on proving to Hitler that he had nothing to fear from them. Invocations and offerings had their cumulative effect: his suppositions crystallized into a conviction. Even at the beginning of November 1937, nay, in February 1938, his preference was still for "the evolutionary course", that is, blackmail and attrition rather than force. But when Schuschnigg seemed about to give him the slip Hitler pounced on Schuschnigg, certain, deep down, that no one would stop him.

On November 10, 1937, Weizsäcker, then head of the Political Department in the German Foreign Office, wrote in anticipation of Lord Halifax's visit:

> For a long time to come, we cannot consider engaging in a war with England. . . . From England we want colonies and freedom of action in the East, from us England wants military quiescence, especially in the West. . . . The British need for tranquillity is

> great. It would be profitable to find out what England would be willing to pay for such tranquillity.

Eliciting was unnecessary. At Berchtesgaden, on November 19, Halifax readily conceded to Hitler the possibility of changes in the European *status quo*, naming Danzig, Austria, and Czechoslovakia — but the changes would have to be effected " by reasonable agreements, and not by force " ; declared Britain's willingness to discuss German colonial claims as part of a general settlement ; and inquired about Hitler's attitude toward the League and disarmament. Such an approach disclosed anxiety and weakness — why then negotiate or offer a *quid pro quo*? Hitler remained intractable and querulous. During the next weeks there was a crescendo of rudeness : Danzig, the Sudetenland, and Austria, asserted the Germans, were not proper subjects for international negotiations ; colonies were a matter of justice, and not a bargaining point ; Germany was courted because of her regained military strength and political freedom of action — the less reason to forgo either ; she would await " concrete ", presumably unconditional, offers. It might " perhaps have been better if Lord Halifax had not come at all ", wrote a high German official analysing his offer.

The following example of the German attitude is but one among many. On January 26, 1938, Henderson called on Neurath ; said he had been to London " for a consultation regarding the steps to be taken by England on the basis of the Halifax conversations " ; " repeated the remark that the British Government, particularly the Prime Minister, was firmly resolved to meet Germany halfway on the colonial question " ; but his task would be made very much easier by " the prospect of some *quid pro quo* on the part of Germany ".

> I told the Ambassador [wrote Neurath] that he had heard repeatedly, and from the mouth of the

> Führer too, that our claim to the return of the colonies could not be the subject of bargaining. The Ambassador went on to ask if we were at least prepared to engage in some discussion of armaments, bombing, &c. I told him that the question of bombing could possibly be discussed independently some time, but in any case not in connexion with the colonial question. When Henderson . . . wanted some assurance that we would eventually discuss the question of re-entry into a reformed League, I declared that I did not wish to discuss this question at all. . . .
>
> Henderson then inquired regarding our plans for Czechoslovakia and Austria. I told him that . . . he knew what complaints we had against Czechoslovakia. . . . As far as Austria was concerned, I could only tell him — and with the request that it be repeated in London — that we would not permit England, either, to interfere in the settlement of our relations with Austria. This settlement was an exclusively German-Austrian question, and we would reject any interference.

This was the kind of language which, *mutatis mutandis*, Henderson was to hear, and accept, during the next twenty months.

Ribbentrop made the same points in London, and received replies and assurances which would have satisfied anyone but a German. After M. Chautemps and M. Delbos, the French Prime Minister and Foreign Minister, had visited London, Mr. Eden informed Ribbentrop that

> he had told the French that the question of Austria was of much greater interest to Italy than to England. Furthermore, people in England recognized that a closer connexion between Germany and Austria would have to come about some time. They wished, however, that a solution by force be avoided.

On December 16 Chamberlain told Ribbentrop that " sentiment in Parliament was favourable toward a settlement with Germany " ; " he eagerly assured me ", wrote Ribbentrop, " that . . . he was not one of those who considered an understanding with Germany to be impossible " ; and said that " the present French Government was better than any of the previous ones ", and that their " sensible attitude had surprised him ".

A fortnight later Ribbentrop declared in a memorandum on German-British relations that he, who had worked " for friendship with England for years ", had " no longer faith in any understanding ".

> A change in the eastern *status quo* to Germany's advantage can only be accomplished by force. . . . France, for all practical purposes, has the power to bring about a German-British war as a result of a German-French conflict. . . . [Such a war] can only be prevented if France *knows from the very beginning* that England's forces would not suffice to guarantee the common victory.

Hence the need of building up a powerful anti-British coalition, by strengthening German friendship with Italy and Japan, and by the inclusion of others.

> We must also continue to foster England's belief that a settlement and an understanding between Germany and England are still possible eventually.

This might restrain England from intervening in a Central European conflict ; yet—

> every day that our political calculations are not actuated by the fundamental idea that England is our most dangerous enemy *would be a gain for our enemies.*

Similarly Weizsäcker in a memorandum, dated December 20, doubted whether " a suitable price can be agreed upon " for an Anglo-German friendship. But, he wrote :

> keeping England in a state of vacillation as long as possible is certainly to be preferred to a condition of definite British hostility toward us.

"Germany is practically the fashion in Paris at present", wrote Weizsäcker on November 23, 1937. M. Bonnet, then Minister of Finance, and the Prime Minister, M. Chautemps, talking to Papen, who visited Paris, pleaded urgently for "a German-French adjustment of interests": but "it was necessary to know the ultimate aims of German policy and to reach an over-all agreement in all spheres". Papen discoursed on

> the Führer's great concept, which had been expressed in his historical decision to declare the German-French border question ended once and for all. If France had thus received full security for her eastern border, it was a natural corollary that she should renounce the balance-of-power policy and stop calling every extension of German influence in the Danube region a threat to French interests.

Bonnet thought that France might "decide on such a policy if she knew the ultimate aims of Germany in the Danube region"; and when asked by Papen whether there would be any objection to a further evolutionary development of the Agreement of July 11, 1936, he "replied definitely in the negative". Similarly Chautemps.

> I was amazed [writes Papen] to note that, like M. Bonnet, the Premier considered a reorientation of French policy in Central Europe as entirely open to discussion . . . he, too, had no objection to a marked extension of German influence in Austria obtained through evolutionary means.

The German Foreign Office thereupon rightly concluded that the French, conscious of their weakened military position, were alarmed at "the growing danger of becoming embroiled in Central Europe", and wanted

> to bargain with Germany for some binding obligations which would restrict the latter's freedom of action in Central and Eastern Europe and thus reduce the risks that they had incurred in these areas through their own policy of alliances.

"What is France . . . . prepared to do in our favour?" wrote Weizsäcker on November 23. "Which of our wishes could and would she fulfil?" Would she stop digging "the spurs into our eastern flank? That is after all the decisive point. . . ." And on December 20:

> We shall not come to an agreement and peaceful relations with France so long as she is not prepared to give up her attempts to threaten Germany from the East by alliances.

The visit of MM. Chautemps and Delbos to London, and in December Delbos's journey to Warsaw and the Little Entente capitals, were watched from Berlin with anxious attention. But the London conference produced nothing new: only appeasement formulas were solemnly reasserted. Thus Eden told the Italian Ambassador that "England and France agreed that in Central Europe (Austria and Czechoslovakia) certain changes could be made, provided . . . that the *status quo* was not changed by force". When on December 3 Delbos was passing through Berlin on his way to Warsaw Neurath greeted him at the railway station and had ten minutes' talk with him.

> He tried to explain to me [writes Neurath] that decided progress had been made in London toward normalizing relations between England, France, and Germany. There had, in particular, been no talk of any intention to block Germany's development again. His trip . . . was not aimed at this in any way, either. . . .
>
> I told M. Delbos that . . . the London communiqué . . . must create the impression that the

> old view-point was still being taken there, namely, of wanting to dictate to Germany how she might pursue her own interests. We rejected this tutelage once and for all.

It was suspected in Berlin that the purpose of Delbos's trip was to win over the small eastern allies "to a general mutual assistance pact with France". But the news that reached the Wilhelmstrasse from the eastern capitals was fully reassuring. The Polish Foreign Minister, Beck, who, in anticipation of Delbos's arrival, had inquired of the Germans about the results of Lord Halifax's visit to Germany, so as "not to be entirely dependent upon the communications of M. Delbos", next informed the German Ambassador that

> Delbos . . . had not, during his stay here, proposed any new groupings for Eastern Europe, in connexion either with Russia or Czechoslovakia . . . a significant fact, which, he presumed, was not devoid of interest for us either. . . . In Rumania Delbos would certainly speak differently, but he would now not find it as easy either as with Titulescu.

In Poland's relations with Czechoslovakia nothing had occurred "that could be considered an improvement". Finally, Beck declared that Poland sincerely desired an improvement in Franco-German relations. And he requested the German Ambassador to transmit his observations to the Reich Foreign Minister.

In Bucharest the Foreign Minister, Antonescu, told the German Minister that "M. Delbos had held out the prospect of initiating an understanding with Germany", and had said that in France 60–80 per cent of the people were for it, especially the youth and the military organizations; that the conversations about a mutual assistance pact had "resulted in nothing new, and that no arrangements of any kind relating to it had been made or were contemplated"; and, unasked, Antonescu reported that

Delbos would use his influence to make Czechoslovakia " settle its relations with Germany by a change of its policy with regard to minorities ". In Belgrade, the Prime Minister, Stoyadinović, " found the eagerness of the representative of the great France really embarrassing ". Delbos told him that, but for the Yugoslav refusal, the Rumanians would have been willing to conclude a mutual assistance pact — " Stoyadinović, smiling, replied that this was typically Antonescu ".

In Prague, the President, the Prime Minister, and the Foreign Minister told the German Minister, Eisenlohr, that agreement had been reached between France and Czechoslovakia to make parallel moves toward a *détente* in their relations with Germany.[1] And Eisenlohr added:

> Beneš had already told me some time ago that, whether developments in Europe would lead once more to the strengthening of the League of Nations, or whether the struggle between the Great Powers would remain the decisive factor in the development of Europe, would determine whether he could seek the security of his country, as hitherto, on a collective basis or would have to follow the example of, say, Yugoslavia, and settle relations with his mighty neighbour by direct negotiations with her.

Here, then, was the man whom, later on, appeasers, about to sacrifice him, chose to depict as obstinate and uncompromising; but who, it was clear, was not going to take the initiative in any action against Germany over Austria. He could have fired the train — and how much the Germans feared it is seen from the pressing assurances they gave to the Czechs at the time of the *Anschluss*.

One further effect of Delbos's round of the East-European allies to the exclusion of Russia was, as the German Ambassador reported from Moscow, to create

[1] *Documents on German Foreign Policy, 1918–1945*, Series D, vol. ii, nos. 30-32, 34, and 38.

"in authoritative circles here a feeling of uneasiness and of being ignored": France seemed to give "Poland priority in the French system of alliances over the Soviet Union".

By the end of the year the German Foreign Office, reviewing the international situation, could state with satisfaction that the territorial *status quo* was no longer excluded from discussion between the Great Powers; that the list of Western desiderata "has obviously shrunk"; that all that remained was a desire for an armaments agreement and the demand that changes should be carried out by peaceful means; and that the Western Powers were turning back to the Four-Power Pact, which implied the isolation of Russia and the loosening up of the "Geneva framework". None the less Weizsäcker wrote on January 10:

> To-day . . . there are no negotiations pending with the Western Powers. It is even questionable whether a workable basis for conversations between us . . . and England and France could be found.

Thus all that the appeasers had achieved by their approaches was to signify to the Germans their own weakness and fears, and to assure Hitler that his further progress in Austria by "evolutionary means" would meet with no objections. He was therefore free to tighten the screw — which he did in his talk with Schuschnigg at Berchtesgaden on February 12. Indeed, on a sober assessment of the situation he might even then have safely proceeded to apply force; seldom, if ever, had there been such unanimity in advance surrender to danger. But perhaps the fears and protests of his generals, who knew Germany to be unready for war, and a lingering disbelief that Europe had sunk so low, had a restraining effect on Hitler. Speaking to a few Nazi leaders from Austria on February 26, he repeated that "he wanted the evolutionary course to be taken".

> The Protocol signed by Schuschnigg was so far-reaching that if completely carried out the Austrian problem would be automatically solved. He did not now desire a solution by violent means, if it could at all be avoided, since the danger for us in the field of foreign policy became less each year and our military power greater each year.

It was still the voice of the anxious generals which spoke through him, not of the man who had got the measure of his opponents. But when Schuschnigg tried to counter Hitler's scheme for Austria's " evolutionary " conquest, Hitler ordered his troops to march ; and only in the afternoon of March 10, 1938, did the Chief of the German General Staff learn that the Austrian frontier would be crossed in the night of March 11-12.

CURTAIN-RAISER TO THE CZECH CRISES OF 1938

Some day Beneš will perhaps be remembered as the man who tried to survive by being reasonable (and plausible) in an age when reason had ceased to count: a Victorian in twentieth-century Central Europe. He lacked President Masaryk's moral authority and philosophic detachment; he had no one to do for him the political house-work, as he had done it for Masaryk; he was in charge of a very difficult establishment. A democrat, both in faith and by nature, he did not tower over other men, but tried to conciliate them, even too readily and too anxiously; he flourished in the League of Nations setting, and was doomed when it collapsed; he was no match for the dictators. But it is time that justice was done to him as a man who strove for peace and at least a measure of decency. When after the Austrian *Anschluss* of March 1938, Czechoslovakia became the object of German pre-aggression manœuvres, and it was found convenient to tax the Czechs with a " fatal hesitation to appreciate the facts " and with remissness " satisfactorily " to settle the Sudeten question, Beneš came in for a great deal of suspicion and blame.

> Although the Czechs may have some reason to distrust the good faith of the German Government [wired Lord Halifax to Mr. Newton, British Minister in Prague, on May 30, 1938], you will appreciate that the latter also doubt the good faith of Dr. Beneš. I fear that this doubt is not wholly unjustified, for whatever truth there may be in suggestion of recent " shufflings " by the Henlein Party, there is no doubt

> that Dr. Beneš has been very reluctant to move for the past two years.

And when Beneš protested against the stories spread about him, and said that it was " an essential condition for his work that he should enjoy confidence ", Halifax remarked:

> In spite of M. Beneš's protest at being suspected of prolonging or postponing a settlement of the Sudetendeutschen question . . . I feel that M. Beneš is still a prisoner of his own past, and that we cannot afford to accept his assurances altogether at their face value.

When in 1940 the B.B.C. played the anthems of the Allied Governments then in England, the Czechoslovak anthem was not played. The Czechs and Beneš remained the scapegoats of the Munichers. To argue would hardly have benefited their cause: Beneš kept silent. He reserved his defence for his memoirs. Of these only the first volume has appeared, and it deals with the years of exile. The entire second volume was to be on Munich, with full documentation in an appendix. Beneš had not completed it before a new catastrophe supervened. He was silenced once more. And it is his two surrenders that are most difficult to defend. To the accusations levelled against him by the appeasers, the second volume of the *Documents on German Foreign Policy*, dealing with Germany and Czechoslovakia, 1937–1938, is sufficient reply — Henlein's rabid diatribes in it as much as the cautious dispatches of the non-Nazi German Minister in Prague, Dr. Eisenlohr. The volume starts with October 8, 1937, but Eisenlohr's report of February 4, 1938, on Czechoslovak domestic policy, supplies a useful retrospect of that " past " which was held up against Beneš.

> In his Reichenberg speech of August 1936 [wrote Eisenlohr], that is, in the first year of his Presidency, President Beneš tried to direct the Sudeten German

> problem into positive channels. His remarks were intended not only to inspire confidence in the Germans, but also as an exhortation to the Czechs. He satisfied neither. The Czechs, because they did not then understand the necessity of concessions. . . . The Germans, because Beneš offered too little. . . .
>
> At the beginning of 1937 Prime Minister Hodža went a step further. He negotiated with the three Activist parties in the Government [1] on the basis of a program put forward by them. . . . The result of the three weeks of negotiation, which ended on February 18, 1937, was . . . laid down in . . . an official announcement by the Government. . . . Its substance was inadequate. . . . Nevertheless, this was only meant as a beginning. Apart from the good intention, perceptible in spite of all caution, the Government were certainly also pursuing the secondary aim of giving fresh impetus to the Activist parties. . . .

The Sudeten German Party, afraid of losing ground if " the Government carried out their intentions " and " the situation of the Sudeten Germans substantially improved as a result of the Activist negotiations ", introduced bills in the Czechoslovak Parliament which, wrote Eisenlohr, though " not the last word in wisdom ", by raising far-reaching demands at that

> critical moment . . . succeeded in weakening the impression of February 18 among the Sudeten German people. This was their primary object.

The basic difference between the Activists and the Sudeten German Party is thus explained by him:

> While . . . all other parties divide the population of the State into horizontal strata, according to their material or religious interests, so that for example German and Czech Social Democrats, or German, Czech and Slovak Agrarians find themselves in the

[1] The German Socialists, Clericals, and Agrarians, who formed part of the Government Coalition and had representatives in the Cabinet.

> same camp to represent their interests, the Sudeten German Party took it upon itself to cut straight across these special interests, to split the population vertically and to gather together all Germans regardless of profession, station, or religion in a common defence against attacks on their national individuality.

Although the Sudeten example threatened the " multinational State " with dismemberment, by February 1937 the European situation forced the Czechoslovak Government to seek contact with the Sudeten German Party; which had now to decide

> whether to persevere . . . in its hitherto unswerving, but also fruitless . . . opposition, or . . . to grasp the proffered hand, take its place at the conference table, and attempt to work for the gradual solution of a problem which, according to Beneš . . . can only be attacked and settled by degrees.

Questioned by Eisenlohr, Henlein replied that

> he needed support . . . from the Reich and therefore must be certain that his decisions harmonized with those of the Reich Government. Above all he must know whether we were still interested in maintaining the fissure between Germans and Czechs, or whether we concurred in the attempt at gradual conciliatory settlement.

Hodža and Henlein met for the first time on September 16, 1937. Hodža argued " that only a gradual development of the minority problem was politically possible ", but he was (as Henlein admits) " courteous and friendly even in heated and ticklish passages ". Henlein, as he states himself, conducted the discussion " with energy and decision "; and he showed little response to the ingratiating advances of Hodža who, " of Slovak origin and Magyar stamp ", claimed " as a former opposition and minority politician " to know " the minority struggle very well ". " The Czechs ", said Hodža, " would have to reduce their demands to the measure due to them": he himself "was honestly desirous of reaching full understanding with the Sudeten German element". "Henlein men were in future to be admitted to the service of the State." He asked Henlein

> to acquaint him with an agent not too much in the public eye who would give him [Hodža] the names of those Henlein people whom he could "smuggle" into civil service posts. "At all events I want to try a big break-through."

Henlein, in turn, demanded

> more decent treatment of the Movement in the future (reference to bans on assemblies and on wearing of jack boots and stockings).

On September 27, Hodža met Schuschnigg at Baden, near Vienna, and early in October, the Czechoslovak Foreign Minister, Dr. Krofta, visited Paris. To Eisenlohr's inquiries about these visits Krofta replied that undue importance was being ascribed by the German Press to the journeys of Czechoslovak Ministers; that he himself "had planned his visit months ago, in order to visit the Exhibition"; but he added that

> the fuss made by the German press over the visit had probably been very agreeable to M. Hodža, because he is pleased when special significance is attributed to his journeys or utterances.

(Reading such effusions, one begins to appreciate the advantages which certain Governments may find in frightening their spokesmen into silence.)

On October 17, 1937, the Sudetens provoked a brawl with the Czech police; a furious anti-Czech campaign was unleashed in Germany; even in the Czechoslovak Foreign Ministry fears were entertained, reported Eisenlohr on October 22, that the incident "might form the starting point for a German-Czechoslovak conflict";

while " even leading personalities of the Sudeten German Party " thought that it might " afford the occasion to bring the Sudeten German question to a head with the help of the Reich ".

> As was learnt in strict confidence by the Legation — and unfortunately not only by them — Konrad Henlein made somewhat similar statements at a conference (*Führerbesprechung*) on the night of October 17-18, and at the same time also expressed the opinion, in virtue of his London talk with Vansittart,[1] that no serious intervention in favour of the Czechs was to be feared from Great Britain and probably also from France.

But the Prague Government adopted from the very outset a conciliatory attitude. And Eisenlohr wired on October 28 :

> I request urgently that German press abstain from attacks on Hodža, who is just now making persevering efforts to settle conflict with Sudeten German Party, and out of excitement over Teplitz incident to find a way back to peaceful development.

On November 9, Eisenlohr had a talk of four hours with Beneš. " His manner ", wrote Eisenlohr, " was natural, friendly, and thoroughly dignified." He was prepared to go a long way to meet the Reich-German demands.

> Even if Beneš's statements were not intended in good faith . . . they would still be of practical importance. . . . I consider, however, his statements to be really true, for . . . the most important condition for the maintenance of the State which he helped to create must be a permanent good relationship to the German people outside and inside the borders of the Czechoslovak State. For this reason I am also inclined to assume that he really wishes to improve the position of the German minority.

[1] Henlein had been in London, October 10-15.

But his task of gaining Czech support for his policy of conciliation would be eased if to the pressure exercised by the Reich was added " the confidence that we have no wish to touch the Czech nation and the Czechoslovak frontiers ". (Four days earlier, in the secret Conference of November 5, Hitler had declared it to be his first objective " to overthrow Czechoslovakia ".)

Henlein, not Eisenlohr, was Hitler's real representative in Czechoslovakia; and in Henlein's " comprehensive survey " of November 19, it is assumed as axiomatic that an understanding between Germans and Czechs in Czechoslovakia was impossible, and that " the de-nationalization and annihilation of the Sudeten Germans " were the aim of Czech policy. And here are some of the claims which Henlein made for his Party:

> The Sudeten Germans are to-day imbued with National Socialist principles and organized in a comprehensive, unitary, National Socialist Party, based on the Führer concept. . . .
>
> The Sudeten German Party has destroyed the fiction of the Czech National State . . . and has materially weakened the political and military value of Czechoslovakia as an ally. . . .
>
> The Sudeten German Party has by its work of political education and organization exorcized the danger of any " Czechoslovakizing " of the Sudeten Germans, that is, of treating them in accordance with the Swiss model (*Verschweizerung*), and has imbued the racial group and their sphere of life with National Socialist principles.
>
> In the face of " democratic " world opinion the Sudeten German Party has given proof that the National Socialist order of leadership and following corresponds with the law of the inner life of the German people. . . .

Still, the Party " must camouflage its profession of National Socialism as an ideology and as a political principle ", and must " outwardly . . . employ democratic terminology and democratic parliamentary methods ". Similarly, while

> at heart it desires nothing more ardently than the incorporation of Sudeten German territory, nay of the whole Bohemian, Moravian, and Silesian area, within the Reich . . . outwardly it must stand for the preservation of Czechoslovakia and for the integrity of its frontiers, and must try to display some apparently genuine aim in the sphere of internal politics to justify its political struggle.

Only by demanding " autonomy ", and not separation,

> was it possible to put the Czechs in the wrong before the world . . . but above all in the eyes of the British.

Commended by Hitler on March 28, 1938, for the " great success " he " has had in England ", and asked to continue the work, Henlein skilfully carried on his game of deception almost to the very end. He visited London about the middle of May, and in a private talk, as reported by Sir Robert (now Lord) Vansittart,[1]

> pointed out how lamentably slow the Czechoslovak Government had been in making any advance ; that he had always been the apostle of conciliation (and I [wrote Vansittart] hastened to assure him that I knew this to be true) but that his position had been rendered almost untenable by the fact that he had so long preached this doctrine without obtaining any appreciable result.

And to Mr. Ashton-Gwatkin, one of Lord Runciman's assistants, he emphatically denied, on August 23, that he " was a dictator ", had any sympathy with " Nazi terror ", or " aimed at political totalitarianism ".[2] " I like him ", wrote Ashton-Gwatkin after that conversa-

[1] *Documents on British Foreign Policy, 1919–1939,* Third Series, vol. i, page 631.

[2] *Ibid.* vol. ii, page 658.

tion in a private letter to Mr. (now Sir William) Strang, who was at that time head of the Central Department of the Foreign Office. " He is, I am sure, an absolutely honest fellow."[1] And on September 6: " An honest unpretentious man ".[2]

" The Sudetendeutsch Party have taken us on ", wrote Ashton-Gwatkin on August 16.[3] (" Taken us in " would have been even more accurate.)[4]

[1] *Ibid.* page 664. [2] *Ibid.* page 669. [3] *Ibid.* page 662.

[4] I have asked Mr. Ashton-Gwatkin, a very old friend, for his comment on this passage. He writes:

> What did I mean by thinking Henlein was " honest "? I believed that he was genuine in his protestations that he was a man of peace, and that it was by peaceful means that he wished to see the Sudetenland obtain a maximum of independence, while remaining within the frontier of Czechoslovakia. In fact, he was not " honest ", because we know now that his " movement " was designed to effect " independence " outside the Czechoslovakian frontier and by incorporation in Germany.
>
> Henlein having obtained his ambition and become a kind of titular President of Sudetenland, was, so I heard, deeply disappointed to find that he was a puppet and not a ruler, and that Frank, his " faithful soldier " (*der treue Soldat*) was given a post of far greater importance. Eventually, like Petronius Arbiter, he opened his veins in a bath, and so died before the Czechs had time to catch and hang him.
>
> I did not dislike Henlein. He was a good-looking chap, hail-fellow-well-met, athletic: his father had been a butcher (in Reichenberg), and himself a bank-clerk: not much education: but a copious flow of flatulent oratory: no political gifts or experience, but chosen as a figure-head by the Sudeten Party and those great landowners who hated the Czechs and feared " bolshevism ".
>
> He was vain, and figured himself to be a great man: but I doubt if he ever had as much influence as it seemed either with the German Nazis or even with his own party.
>
> " The bold Bohemian, in an evil hour,
> Treads the dread summits of Caesarian power."
>
> My instructions from Lord Halifax and Sir R. Vansittart, were to cultivate Henlein, and see whether some composition between Sudetens and Czechs might not be possible. It was quite possible, if it had not been for Hitler and the Nazis. We (Runciman Mission with approval of the F.O.) therefore urged Henlein to go to Hitler and explain that he was now getting everything he wanted, so let there be peace. Henlein went (with an appalling cold!). He was not an effective messenger: we now know why. I doubt whether Hitler at any time regarded Henlein as anything more than a useful stooge. I doubt if we could have known that at the time. In any case, the whole idea of the Runciman Mission was based on the assumption that freedom of negotiation between Czechs and Sudetens was possible.

Halifax's visit to Germany and Delbos's tour of Eastern Europe, in November-December 1937, made attention centre on the international situation. Czechoslovakia continued towards Germany her policy of conciliation, or even " appeasement ", interlarded with unduly familiar confidences by both Krofta and Hodža to the German Minister. On December 9, speaking about the coming visit of Delbos, Krofta denied that " any further treaty obligations " were contemplated. " The plan of a general pact of assistance between the Little Entente and France was torpedoed ", and early in November Beneš had told King Carol of Rumania " that Czechoslovakia no longer pursued that plan ". And, " with the urgent request for the strictest secrecy on all matters which concerned his Prime Minister ", Krofta added the following explanation of some recent moves: Hodža " wavered between the desire to reach an understanding with Germany at any price, and sudden attacks of panic because of Germany "; terrified by some reports received in September, he raised with the French the question of widening the Franco-Czech treaty; but Krofta expounded in Paris both Hodža's view and " his own divergence from it ". It all finished with a speech by Delbos " in very general terms ", which did not even name Czechoslovakia.

> Beneš, too, who had not at first wished to prevent Hodža's excitable activities, as he could not always be putting the brake on him, had been extremely satisfied that the affair had taken this peaceful course.

Could any German wish for a more ingenuous and loquacious Czech Foreign Minister? (Krofta was to die in 1946 as a result of rigours suffered during the war in a German concentration camp.)

No less communicative was Hodža.

> The decisive political discussion between Delbos and Beneš [wrote Eisenlohr on December 17] is taking place to-day at a private luncheon party at Lany,[1] where presumably no one besides Hodža and Krofta will be present. Hodža has promised to inform me confidentially next week of the result, as far as he is able.

Hodža was not present, but the same evening, at a reception in the French Legation, Beneš hastened to inform Eisenlohr

> that Delbos's visit had passed off satisfactorily, France desired a *détente* with us and desired likewise that Czechoslovakia might achieve good relations with the Reich. This was fully in accordance with his own view.

The theme was further developed by both Hodža and Krofta with appropriate indiscretions, even concerning Beneš.

And here are a few salient points from Eisenlohr's survey of " Czechoslovak Foreign Policy in 1937 ". " The treaty relationship with Soviet Russia . . . has paled." With France it " has remained unaltered ", but there is " the alarming uncertainty " whether, in view of German rearmament and fortifications, " French military assistance, if it came, would not come too late ". France's authority as a Great Power is shaken. Poland continues to show " cool reserve toward Czech wooing ". Both Beneš and Krofta view sceptically the " Hodža plan " for " a politico-economic linking together of the Danubian States by means of a kind of preferential system ", and it was not mentioned " by either at the visit of the French Foreign Minister to Prague ". Nothing was done in 1937 to establish closer relations with Austria, " because the Czechoslovak Government wish to, and must, avoid

[1] The official country residence of the President of Czechoslovakia.

everything that would arouse mistrust in Berlin ".[1] " The *Anschluss* is still feared in Prague now as before; if it happened, not a finger could be raised to prevent it by their own efforts."

> The establishment of permanently good relations with the German Reich has become for Czechoslovakia the most important and vital question . . . everyone in this land knows to-day that a friendly relationship with Germany can alone guarantee State and national self-determination.

It is further realized, wrote Eisenlohr, that a *rapprochement* with Germany has to be purchased with concessions to the Sudeten Germans, and Beneš, Hodža, and Krofta alike are endeavouring to remove causes of conflict " wherever possible in order to pave the way to a secure future ". And he added: " A certain measure of success had not been denied them ".

> With a *détente* between the Western and the Axis Powers, the moment long and patiently awaited by Beneš seems to be approaching when he can alter his foreign policy without appearing to alter it, when he, by participating in the conciliatory move by France and Britain, could keep their sympathy or assistance, and simultaneously transfer the centre of gravity of his policy to the good relationship with Germany which is to be hoped for.

And as the Sudeten problem is the one obstacle to " the desired *rapprochement* with Germany ":

[1] Nevertheless Hitler, in his letter to Mussolini of March 11, 1938, quoted a marked *rapprochement* between Czechoslovakia and Austria as one of his main reasons for taking action:

> In recent months I have seen, with increasing preoccupation, how a relationship was gradually developing between Austria and Czechoslovakia which, while difficult for us to endure in peace-time, was bound, in case of a war imposed upon Germany, to become a most serious threat to the security of the Reich.

> I consider it probable that in this matter he will make any concessions which do not jeopardize the unity of his Government . . .

Indeed, even if no *détente* was achieved between the Four Powers, Beneš, wrote Eisenlohr,

> will nevertheless seek a gradual *rapprochement* to us, provided we make this in the slightest degree possible.

(Though ready to attune himself to Hitler's wishes, Eisenlohr was not out to destroy Czechoslovakia; and Hitler, when discussing with Keitel on April 21, 1938, how to proceed against the Czechs, thought that having, if necessary, Eisenlohr assassinated in Prague might create a suitable " incident ".)

On February 8, Sudeten representatives met Hlinka, the Slovak separatist leader: Eisenlohr warned Berlin that encouraging the Slovak Autonomists " gives the impression that we wish to disintegrate and destroy the Czechoslovak State ". Next, on February 11-12, Sudeten leaders saw the Hungarian Minister for Minorities who " made no secret of Hungary's efforts to contribute to Czechoslovakia's disappearance from the map of Europe "; while the Hungarian Prime Minister and the Foreign Minister told them " that Budapest and Warsaw were of the same mind in regard to the political fate of Czechoslovakia ". But on March 4 a Hungarian suggestion to Berlin to resume discussing " possible war aims *vis-à-vis* Czechoslovakia ", met with an evasive reply: the Austrian crisis was under way, and it mattered to the Germans to avoid Czech intervention. Göring, on March 11, declared " on his word of honour " to Mastny, Czechoslovak Minister in Berlin, " that there was not the least reason for Czechoslovakia to feel any anxiety ", and " that Germany was desirous of continuing policy toward Czechoslovakia of improving mutual relations ". The same night he repeated these assurances on behalf of

Hitler; and next day, both he and Neurath (in Ribbentrop's absence again in charge of the German Foreign Office) reiterated them once more. Eisenlohr wrote that day from Prague:

> M. Masařik [an official of the Czechoslovak Foreign Office] . . . told me that Field Marshal Göring's statements would be used with a certain irony by the Foreign Ministry in reassuring those Ministers of foreign Powers who were inquiring anxiously about the fate of Czechoslovakia.

To profess faith where none is due, is one of the pitiable ways in which the weak try to propitiate or pin down the strong.

To sum up. It was the aim of Beneš to establish a real community between Czechs and Germans within Czechoslovakia: ultimately a common "territorial" nationality. Such "Czechoslovakizing" — treatment on "the Swiss model" — was to the Sudeten German Party an "attack on their national individuality". They countered it by "splitting the population vertically"; and Germany was interested "in maintaining the fissure between Germans and Czechs". Beneš further aimed at an understanding with Germany, if possible under the wing of the Western Powers: so as to prevent it from turning into vassalage. There was no response from Germany, except assurances given at the height of the Austrian crisis, and explained away as soon as it had passed. Now the stage was set for Czechoslovakia's annihilation.

THE MAKERS OF MUNICH

In the Chancellery conference of November 5, 1937, Hitler pointed to the annexation of Austria and Czechoslovakia as his first objective; it was his " unalterable resolve " to settle the problem of Germany's *Lebensraum* " at the latest by 1943–45 ", or earlier should France become immobilized by " internal strife " or by war with another Power. A paralysis of the French will or the British mind so complete and suicidal as to make them deliver to him his victims, and with them the strategic key-position in Central Europe, he dimly anticipated,[1] but as yet did not dare to name, perhaps not even to himself, as a third, early opening for action; nor did others think it possible till it actually happened. And still, the fatal *dénouement* of Munich was predetermined, not so much by the concrete facts of the actual situation, as by the notions, velleities, preconceived ideas, and obsessions of the main actors: each of them comes on to the stage with his set piece which runs its course, organically unaffected by the unfolding scene. The published British and German documents for the half-year from March to September 1938, cover about 2000 large pages, a vast record[2]— yet for how much do inquiry and argument, notes, directives, reports, and speculations count in the end? Men seem to search and grope for solutions; but when hesitant they are often merely obstinate and obtuse; most of them finish by doing exactly what they had been intent on

[1] See above, page 124.

[2] *Documents on British Foreign Policy, 1919–1939*, E. L. Woodward and Rohan Butler, assisted by Margaret Lambert (Editors), Third Series, vols. i and ii, 1948 and 1949; and *Documents on German Foreign Policy, 1918–1945*. Series D (1937–1945), vol. ii, *Germany and Czechoslovakia, 1937–1938* (1949).

from the outset. The teetotums spin and hum; he who could gauge how they are set could foretell the future; and a good deal of melancholy amusement can be obtained from tracing it *ex post.*

The future was forecast in November 1937. A fortnight after Hitler's secret conference, which marked "the transition to planned aggression", the British Government signified to him their readiness to concede changes in the territorial *status quo* of Central Europe provided they were effected "by reasonable agreements and not by force". And in the course of the next ten months it was clearly conveyed to him that the British Government had no interest in Czechoslovakia; that they were prepared to demand the most far-reaching sacrifices from her "if only Germany would adhere to peaceful methods"; that almost anything which Germany could obtain in Czechoslovakia without firing a shot, would have their approval; but that an armed conflict had to be avoided at all cost, for France would probably become involved, and then Great Britain might not be able to stay out. In that same month of November, leading French Ministers told the Germans that France would be prepared to consider a reorientation of her policy in Central Europe and "a Franco-German adjustment of interests"; from which the Germans rightly concluded that France, alarmed at "the growing danger of becoming embroiled in Central Europe", wished to reduce the risks she had incurred through her alliances in that region.[1] And gradually it became obvious that she was prepared to see almost any solution imposed on the Czechs: about May 15, 1938, M. Bonnet begged Lord Halifax "to save France from the cruel dilemma of dishonouring her Agreements or becoming involved in war"; on May 26, he told the German Ambassador that if the Czechs proved unyielding, France would inform them that she would have to recon-

[1] See above, pages 129-30.

sider her treaty obligations; and on September 2, that the Czechs would be forced to accept Runciman's verdict, which, in all probability, would concede 70-90 per cent of the Sudeten demands. By September 13, according to the British Ambassador in Paris, Bonnet seemed "completely to have lost his nerve", and was "ready for any solution to avoid war". Hitler, for his part, was determined all along to smash Czechoslovakia if he could do so without having to fight the Western Powers. Munich gave to each of the three Governments what they were determined to secure; and the agreement was received (at least outwardly) with greater enthusiasm in London and Paris than in Berlin.

The component elements in the situation could be discerned before the issue was joined; but could they be carried, undisturbed, to their logical term? — a solution so grotesque and revolting that no one would have dared openly to suggest it at the outset. No man could have planned the course. But each actor in his own way contributed to the success of German blackmail. The British Government tried to elicit from Berlin what concessions would satisfy them. Thus, in an *aide-mémoire* of May 11:

> If His Majesty's Government are to use their influence in Prague they must have some idea of the terms that would be likely, from the German point of view, to form the basis of an agreed settlement.

But the Germans gave the stock reply that this was a matter for direct negotiation between the Sudetens and Prague. And yet the British Government, with the Germans uncommitted to any solution, were putting relentless pressure on Beneš to catch up with the ever-rising Sudeten demands: he was told to attempt "a comprehensive settlement"; to make "a generous offer"; "to go to the limit and beyond in meeting the wishes of the Sudetens"; "to do more and more and more to meet them"; "to accept great sacrifices and even considerable risks ". But the British Government themselves, when asked by the Czechs what concessions they would consider adequate, were as evasive as the Germans. They were careful not to commit themselves to any particular plan " which might not prove acceptable to the German Government ", and from which they might next have " to run away . . . because the Germans rejected it and became violent again ".

Therefore Runciman was sent as " an independent mediator " for whom H.M. Government disclaimed all responsibility ; none the less, Halifax would convey to him how undesirable it would be for him to draw up any scheme savouring of arbitration, or to " pronounce judgment " which might prove embarrassing to H.M. Government. And in a letter to Henderson, on August 5 : " We must . . . be very careful that he [Runciman] does not take any action " which would commit this country still further to oppose Germany should she resort to force. Halifax thought that Great Britain could contract out of the moral obligations implicit in the part assumed by her. But the Czechs refused to believe that, after having exercised such extreme pressure, she could do so and see their country " sacrificed as the result of following the proffered advice ". Thus, in August, a Czech said to the British Military Attaché :

> . . . you English possess a powerful weapon to a degree which no other country enjoys, and that is your national prestige. That prestige is only partially based on your resources ; it derives its real strength from your high moral standards in public life and policy. A single departure from those standards would mean moral suicide for you and disaster for the rest of the world.

Munich was such a departure ; but nothing is either so final as people assume at the time, or so transient as they later think it to have been.

The liquidation of Austria opened up the problem of Czechoslovakia. The solemn assurances given to the Czechs by Berlin on March 11 and 12 were explained to have merely meant that " on the occasion of military action in Austria the Czechoslovak frontier would be respected ". On March 28 Henlein, leader of the Sudetens (since 1935 in German pay), was received by Hitler. He was told that their problem would be settled in the near future; that they should not accept Czech promises, but by a " step-by-step specification of demands . . . avoid entry into the Government "; and " always demand so much that they could never be satisfied ". He was praised for " the great success " he had achieved in London, asked to go there again, and to use his influence to ensure non-intervention by Great Britain.

The *Anschluss* lashed Sudeten fervour into frenzy; an early entry of German troops was expected; Henlein's war standard was hoisted; crowds marched shouting " One people, one Reich, one Führer ". " On orders from above ", wrote the German Minister, Dr. Eisenlohr, from Prague on March 31, " Czechoslovak police and *gendarmerie* showed great restraint ", which was interpreted by the Sudetens as an " abdication of civil authority ". But Germany's military and diplomatic preparations were as yet incomplete: Berlin therefore ordered " the natural enthusiasm of the population " to be kept " within bounds dictated by political necessity ". On April 24 the Congress of the S.D.P. (*Sudeten Deutsche Partei*) met at Carlsbad; Henlein spoke of the " inalienable right to self-determination "; and, in eight deliberately vague points, put forward a program for a virtual transformation of the Sudeten territory into a Nazi preserve. Vagueness, he subsequently told Runciman, left room for compromise; in truth, for the prescribed raising of terms. By the time fear of Hitler had made the Runciman Mission discover that the Carlsbad program was " not unreasonable ", and the British Minister pressed it on Beneš, " his difficulty ", replied Beneš, was " that no one could tell him what it really meant . . . he would in fact be signing a blank cheque ".

One of the most deplorable features was the confidence and sympathy shown to Henlein by London. He came again on May 13, having seen *en route* Ribbentrop, whom he told he would " deny in London that he is acting on instructions from Berlin ". This he did upon " his word of honour " ; said that local autonomy was his aim ; and claimed to have " always been the apostle of conciliation ", foiled by the Czech Government which was " lamentably slow in making any advance ". A fortnight later he sent one of his " private messages ", to which Halifax immediately reacted, coming down heavily on Beneš. Henlein got worried, and inquired in Berlin :

> What attitude should I adopt if the Czechs, under foreign pressure, suddenly accede to all my demands and present, as a counter-demand, entry into the Government ?

He himself proposed the following :

> If the Czechs yield on all points, I shall answer " Yes ", with the demand that the foreign policy of Czechoslovakia be modified. The Czechs would never accede to that.

Since the time when Beneš became President in 1936, he had sincerely endeavoured to improve relations with the Sudetens and the Reich (this was repeatedly admitted by the German Legation in Prague) ;[1] of the Prime Minister, Dr. Hodža, it was said by the Sudetens themselves, that he set his " whole ambition " on being able, some day, to claim merit for a Czech-Sudeten agreement ; whereas Henlein boasted in Berlin of having prevented a settlement of Czechoslovakia on the Swiss model (*Ver-*

[1] See above, pages 136 and 146-7.

schweizerung).[1] But in public, naturally, no credit was given to the Czechs for concrete concessions and far-reaching measures of conciliation; their attempts at serious negotiations were evaded, or negotiations, when started, broken off for trivial, trumped-up reasons; while the same hackneyed story was successfully retailed over and over again in London: the Czechs are pig-headed and obdurate; unwilling to make reasonable concessions; those they make are wholly inadequate; Beneš does not mean business, his promises are worthless, he plays for time and cheats, and must be "forced"; but the effect of "the so-called British and French pressure on Prague" is nil; "the attitude of the Prague Government has merely increased in intransigence and aggressiveness"; they count on British and French support, and mean to provoke war. The Sudetens, it was said in August, cannot wait indefinitely, nor the German Government stand aside: Hitler will be forced to act.

On April 20, Hitler discussed Czechoslovakia with Keitel. Not to shock world opinion, he rejected a "strategic surprise attack without cause or justification", but envisaged action after diplomatic preparation or as the result of an "incident". Hence the interim directive of May 20 did not propose

> to smash Czechoslovakia by military action in the immediate future without provocation, unless an unavoidable development of political conditions *within* Czechoslovakia forces the issue, or political events in Europe create a particularly favourable opportunity which may perhaps never recur.

But that same day the Czechs, apprehending an imminent German attack, called up some reservists; Britain warned Germany against precipitate action; and the impression got about that Hitler had suffered a check. Two months

[1] See above, page 141.

later, Nevile Henderson, effective only in putting himself "under the German skin", spoke of the feeling "that Hitler has allowed himself to be impudently defied by Beneš and his miserable little nation": "the slap in the face of May 21" had to be "obliterated". Hitler declared in his Directive "Green" of May 30:

> It is my unalterable decision to smash Czechoslovakia by military action in the near future. It is the business of the political leadership to await or bring about the suitable moment from a political and military point of view.

In the meantime propaganda warfare was to "intimidate the Czechs by means of threats and wear down their power of resistance". And in the "General Strategic Directive" of June 18:

> The settlement of the Czech question by my own free decision stands as the immediate aim in the forefront of my political intentions. I am resolved, as from October 1, 1938, onwards, to make use of every favourable political opportunity for the realization of this aim. . . . I shall, however, only decide to take action against Czechoslovakia if, as in the case of the occupation of the demilitarized zone and the entry into Austria, I am firmly convinced that France will not march and therefore Britain will not intervene either.

On that head the Western Powers amply reassured him in the course of the next months (they also helped him to wear down Czech power of resistance). It was therefore decided at the end of August:

> Operation "Green" will be set in motion by an incident in Czechoslovakia, which will provide Germany with a pretext for military intervention.
>
> The fixing of the time of this incident *to the day and hour* is of the utmost importance. It must take place in general weather conditions favourable for our superior Luftwaffe to go into action . . . no

advance measures may be taken before X-day minus 1, which cannot be innocently explained, as otherwise the incident would appear to have been staged by us.

But the German Army Command were convinced that they could not as yet risk war with the Western Powers. General Beck, C.G.S., wrote that action on the lines of Hitler's directive of May 30 would be fatal, and that the General Staff declined responsibility for it. On July 16 he declared once more that a major war was bound to result in " all-round catastrophe " for Germany, and that Hitler should be made to " postpone solving the Czech problem by force till the military situation was radically changed " — a view shared by all those " who would have to deal with the preparation and conduct of a war against Czechoslovakia ". Early in August Brauchitsch summoned a conference of commanding generals; Beck read out his memorandum of July 16; General Adam, commander-designate of the western front, spoke of the utter insufficiency of its fortifications and forces (five active and four reserve divisions and some *Landwehr*); all present except two agreed in opposing war; but Beck alone resigned in protest.[1] On September 26 the generals once more tried to dissuade Hitler; and so did Grand Admiral Raeder. But then none of them could imagine that the Western Powers would abandon Czechoslovakia, still less hold her down for the executioner.

The British Government were not ignorant of the situation and the view the German generals took of it. The British Military Attaché in Berlin wrote on July 28 that he was continually " coming across evidence that Germany as a whole is not ready for war this autumn ", and that the Army Command were definitely opposed to it. During the next two months German staff officers, " obviously perturbed ", repeatedly told him how much

[1] See above, pages 30-32.

the Army deprecated Hitler's military preparations. On August 21 the Head of the Attaché Group let it be understood that, failing a solution of the Sudeten question,

> the German General Staff had only one besetting doubt and ground for perturbation, and this lay in their uncertainty as to Britain's reaction to direct action.

Even Göring, reported the Berlin Embassy on September 11, did not " regard Germany's prospects in a general war too optimistically ". On August 18, Ewald von Kleist came to London,[1] sent by the generals: they were " all dead against war ", but unable to stop it without help and encouragement from outside. Again, on the 21st, he told the British Military Attaché in Berlin:

> The German General Staff are staggered by the fact that the German mobilization is being taken so quietly abroad. . . . There is everywhere terror at the prospect of a catastrophe.

And Carl Burckhardt,[2] on September 5: " the only hope of peace " lay in Chamberlain telling Hitler " that if Czechoslovakia were attacked England would support her with all forces at her command ". But such appeals were dismissed by Chamberlain as anti-Nazi propaganda.

Indeed, even Nevile Henderson, the arch-appeaser, on August 6, expressed to Halifax the belief " that if we really showed our teeth, Hitler would not dare to make war to-day ". And on August 19: " I believe if we saw any utility in war, now would be the moment to make it rather than later ". But on August 22:

> Have we or have we not got to fight Germany again? The followers of the Crowe tradition in your Department argue . . . that it is inevitable. I regard that attitude as nothing short of disastrous.

Practical negotiations for an Anglo-German understanding, he wrote on August 12, were possible only after a solution of the Sudeten problem.

[1] See above, pages 32-3. [2] See above, page 76.

> An Anglo-German understanding means world peace for a generation at least. Are we to prejudice this prospect out of a sentiment for a Czechoslovakia which was constitutionally and initially a mistake?

This, indeed, was in a nutshell the thesis of Chamberlain and his circle. " Czechoslovakia is, and will remain, a thorn in Chamberlain's flesh ", wrote Jan Masaryk on July 14, 1938, " and his dislike of us will not grow less." [1] And the German Ambassador, Dirksen, on July 5: " Chamberlain is committed to the idea of European settlement with all the obstinacy which is characteristic of his family ". He firmly believed in the possibility of a comprehensive agreement with the dictators, and thought himself called upon to achieve it: " my policy of general appeasement ". He was unversed in foreign politics, unimaginative, unconscious of his own limitations, rigid and doctrinaire. His reference, on September 27, to the " quarrel in a far-away country between people of whom we know nothing ", truly expressed his own feelings. He knew little about Austria, Czechoslovakia, or Danzig, and cared even less: the political and strategic importance of those countries, occasionally admitted, never really entered his purview. They were to him tiresome side-issues, which could easily be settled " by peaceful evolution ", once confidence was re-established between the nations, foremost between Britain and Germany. Even at Berchtesgaden he thought he would be able to begin " the conversation with a general consideration of Anglo-German relations ". He had made up for himself a conception of Hitler, of his schemes and intentions; and he adhered to it whatever the evidence against it. For a long time he refused to believe that Hitler meant to destroy Czechoslovakia; and when told by him at Berchtesgaden, with much ranting against the Czechs,

[1] See F. Berber, *Europäische Politik, 1933–1938, im Spiegel der Prager Akten* (1942), Third Edition, page 116.

that after he and others had obtained the territories they claimed, what was left of that country "would be so small that he would not bother his head about it", Chamberlain accepted his word as security for the nation which was being destroyed. At Munich Hitler's proposals agreeably surprised him "by the degree of latitude they left to the International Commission" which was to draw the frontiers after Czechoslovakia had been disarmed. Even then he understood nothing. "Later", writes M. Coulondre, "whenever my colleague Henderson talked to me on that subject [of the International Commission], which he did not like to mention, he would blush."[1]

Halifax had less trust in Hitler. But his major aim, too, was to avert a European war, at whatever cost to the Czechs. Czechoslovakia was the weaker side, and Hitler was aggressive: he had therefore to be placated. Halifax himself said to Ribbentrop on the day of Hitler's ultimatum to Austria, that

> public opinion . . . would inevitably ask . . . what there was to prevent the German Government from seeking to apply in similar fashion naked force to the solution of their problems in Czechoslovakia or to any other in which they thought it might be useful.

And he best answered his own question in a letter to Henderson on August 5:

> I find it difficult to believe that, *if they were convinced that it meant a general war*, they would think it worth while to try and insist by force on their full desiderata for Czechoslovakia, whatever these may be. Indeed I would have guessed that if they were so convinced, they would in fact find means of putting up, with good or ill grace, with a great deal less.

[1] Robert Coulondre, *De Staline à Hitler: souvenirs de deux ambassades, 1936–1939* (1950), page 172.

He therefore wished " to get it into the very stupid heads of the Germans " that it was dangerous for them to " step on the spring ".

> It is our only chance as I see it of preventing them doing it, and it is a difficult line to ride, without exposing ourselves to humiliation if we don't go to war.

But indeed, as he put it elsewhere, the British Government were not prepared " to enter upon hostilities with Germany on account of aggression by Germany on Czechoslovakia ". None the less, they should, he thought, do everything in their power

> to keep the Germans guessing and prevent them from thinking that the danger of any extension of hostilities arising from the use of force by them against Czechoslovakia was in any way negligible.

But a raving maniac is not easily " kept guessing ", nor is the intricate bluff of equivocal declarations possible where numbers of men are engaged ; least of all, with a man like Nevile Henderson for ambassador.

On August 5, Halifax wrote to Henderson :

> Nothing that any of us ever say or do ought to give any tittle of encouragement to the Germans to believe that the danger of British intervention is negligible.

But that same day, Henderson told them " that Great Britain would not think of risking one sailor or airman for Czechoslovakia ". Nor was this an exceptional performance on his part. Warnings which he was instructed to give, he would invalidate by gratuitously identifying himself with the German attitude. To the Germans themselves he would describe their military preparations as " understandable defence measures ". And when a grave appeal from Chamberlain and Halifax to Hitler concerning those preparations was turned down on a technicality, Henderson confided to the German Foreign Office "that he, too, did not consider the method [adopted by his own Government] correct". He would inveigh before the Germans against "Beneš's methods" and express "his aversion to the Czechs in very strong terms". Intent on ingratiating himself with Hitler and Ribbentrop, he earned their contempt, and was treated as no other ambassador. Coulondre writes that on Hitler "la présence ou la parole de Sir Nevile Henderson avait pour effet curieux de le mettre en rage";[1] and Henderson himself found that for his meetings with Hitler the moment was always "ill-chosen" — Hitler "in a vile temper" and making "no effort to conceal it".[2]

Henderson's communications to London, though they naturally omit or attenuate his disastrous "confidences" to the Germans, contain enough to prove him unsuited for ambassador. Conceited, vain, self-opinionated, rigidly adhering to his preconceived ideas, he poured out telegrams, dispatches, and letters in unbelievable numbers and of formidable length, repeating a hundred times the same ill-founded views and ideas. Obtuse enough to be a menace, and not stupid enough to be innocuous, he proved *un homme néfaste* — important, because he echoed and reinforced Chamberlain's opinions and policy. In that sense he was representative; and this is the explanation why, opposed to what he called to Halifax "your Department", he was continued in Berlin. He helped to baulk whatever feeble attempts were made to stand up to Hitler, and was one of the chief artificers of Munich. At the end of July he painted a picture of a Four-Power Conference to settle the fate of Czechoslovakia, with Russia excluded. Henderson was told by the Foreign Office that "keeping Russia out of Europe altogether" was "not an aspect of German policy which we wish to encourage";

[1] *Op. cit.* page 175.

[2] *Failure of a Mission*, pages 42, 49, and 114.

yet he saw his scheme realized two months later exactly as he had sketched it, and with results he had long advocated. He was one of the very few who had early knowledge of Chamberlain's intention to fly to Germany; and naturally greatly encouraged it.

In the 1250 large pages of the British pre-Munich documents, the question of Europe's political and strategic configuration after Czechoslovakia had been obliterated is nowhere dealt with: amazing mental reticence. It is discussed with deep anxiety by M. Daladier and officials of the Quai d'Orsay; on the British side a blind wall is raised against the future, at least by those vocal in the documents. All they know is that war must be averted. The Germans cannot be stopped from overrunning Czechoslovakia, nor could she be re-created in her present frontiers — why "fight a European war for something you cannot protect, and do not expect to restore"? (Six months later Poland was encouraged to resist.) The British people will not wage war to prevent the Sudetens from joining the Reich (why then to prevent Danzig?). An attempt to do so would meet with opposition at home and in the Dominions (the facts and exigencies of the situation were never put to either by men who failed or refused to see them). Hitler (admittedly "an individual of peculiar temperament", "pathological", or even "half mad") is to be deprived of "reasonable" grievances, and to be "taken at his word" (which he had never kept). Russia's support for Czechoslovakia (whose ally she was) was discounted (but next was solicited for the Poland of the "Riga Line"). Even the argument that this country needed time to rearm is deprived of validity by the change in the balance of armaments and forces which the loss of Czechoslovakia was bound to produce. In truth, neither side was ready for a major war in 1938, either militarily or morally; but while in the West there was genuine horror of renewed bloodshed, in

Germany there was only fear of a war they might lose. When between Berchtesgaden and Godesberg, German public opinion became convinced that the Western Powers would not fight but that Czechoslovakia would resist, an " improvement in national morale ", as Henderson called it, immediately set in :

> . . . fear and dislike of war have almost disappeared [he telegraphed on September 19]. Indeed in some circles prospect of punitive expedition against the Czechs seems to be looked forward to with pleasurable anticipation.

What amazes in the German documents is the conviction, contrary to evidence yet almost universal among German diplomatists, that the Western Powers would fight. But people think in stereotypes : and these depicted a different France and Britain — of Clemenceau, Poincaré, and Foch, of Grey, Lloyd George, and Churchill. Hitler alone banked on the moral collapse of the Western Powers. Was it because he had had no practical experience of dealing with the other France and Britain, or because the conclusion which at the time of Munich proved correct coincided with his wishes and gave free rein to his passions ? Anyhow, the initiative lay entirely with him ; he knew that the Western Powers would not attack him, and he could therefore play on their fears ; and, being a sadist and a gambler, he did not recoil from the risks never absent from such a crisis (but even on September 5 Henderson still doubted whether the forces working for war " will overcome Hitler's own love for peace, dislike of dead Germans and hesitation of risking his régime on a gambler's throw "). For there was the risk of the Western Powers having to act, after all, in accordance with the modes and customs of an earlier period : unless the ruts run in the desired direction even fear may not prevail. But new ruts had been provided by the habits and shams of the inter-war period (" diplomacy by conference ", " full, frank, and friendly conversations ", article 19 of the League Covenant, " freely negotiated agreements ", etc.) and these served Chamberlain in his desire to seek a personal interview with Hitler — an idea, he said, " so unconventional and daring that it rather took Halifax's breath away "— and to carry through his policy, which takes away the breath of the reader.

It would serve no purpose to attempt telling in brief the story even of the Runciman Mission, " peace-makers " who became the pace-makers of Munich ; still less of the crucial fortnight, September 15-29, which in the British documents alone fills 300 pages. The broad outlines were visible even at the time ; and what is revealed by detail can only be shown and tasted in detail ; but it will take a book to examine, one by one, the stones with which the road to Munich was paved. Every man continued along the line he had followed during the past six months — except that the movement gathered vertiginous speed and a ghastly momentum. In the previous long-drawn process of attrition there was time and room for disguise and make-believe (flimsy though it did prove). But in the violent rush down the precipice things appear with glaring starkness ; promises and guarantees vanish overnight ; sacrifices are inflicted on the Czechs to preserve them, so they are told, from even worse ones, which in turn are demanded from them almost before they had time fully to envisage the former. And then the Munich conference, for which Hitler had given Mussolini directions and Chamberlain gave him thanks. Daladier and Chamberlain were treated with an inattention bordering on contempt : but Chamberlain apparently never noticed it ; and having delivered Czechoslovakia, land and men, into Hitler's hands he took his stand on trifles most truly within his range : claims to compensation arising from ceded State property, currency, outstanding loans, etc. The business man and administrator was winding up a broken concern. Of the "pity and fear" of that night he felt nothing. When all was over, and at 1.30 A.M. the two Prime Ministers had to inform the Czech representatives of the death verdict passed on their nation, unheard, Daladier was visibly embarrassed while Chamberlain "yawned without ceasing and with no show of embarrassment" — how little he realized what they had done can be seen from his previous suggestion that Daladier "should take the Agreement to Prague".

Next morning Chamberlain went to see Hitler. They had "a very friendly and pleasant talk" about Spain and a possible Four-Power conference, about the burden of armaments and bombing from the air, about international trade, German economic relations with South-Eastern Europe, and loans required to facilitate the flow of goods in both directions — and:

> Now, he would not keep Herr Hitler any longer, but he wished to say that he thought it would be a pity if this meeting passed off with nothing more than the settlement of the Czech question, which had been agreed upon yesterday. What he had in mind was to suggest to Herr Hitler that it would be helpful to both countries and to the world in general if they could issue some statement which showed the agreement between them on the desirability of better Anglo-German relations, leading to a greater European stability. Accordingly, he had ventured to draft a short statement which he would now ask Herr Hitler to read and to consider whether he would be disposed to issue such a statement over the signatures of himself and the Prime Minister to the public. As these observations were translated to Herr Hitler he ejaculated at intervals "Ja! Ja!" and when it was finished he said he would certainly agree to sign this document. When did the Prime Minister wish to do so?

> The Prime Minister: Immediately.
>
> Herr Hitler: Then let us sign.
>
> At this point they both rose, went to a writing table and, without any further words, appended their signatures to the document.

With this document Chamberlain returned in triumph to London.

MEMOIRS OF A REALIST

M. ROBERT COULONDRE was French Ambassador in Moscow from November 1936 till October 1938 and next in Berlin, where he remained till the outbreak of war.

> Veritable acrobatics were enjoined on me! After having gone to Moscow to work for an understanding against Hitler, I was now to proceed to Berlin to work for an understanding with Hitler.

Diplomate de carrière, he pursued the policy laid down by his Government; but he preserved his freedom of judgment and advised them accordingly: no European diplomatist comes out better from the ordeal of those years than M. Coulondre, and it is through no fault of his own that he has now to register a double failure. He tells the story with lucid objectivity and dispassionate frankness, unaffected by subsequent developments which are irrelevant to it, and indifferent to the reactions which those developments have evoked. Trimmers, great or small, who anxiously adjust their view of the past to the hour they write in, are as unfit to record events as they are, as a rule, to mould them.

" From the first day ", writes Coulondre, " I was a whole-hearted supporter of the Franco-Soviet Pact."[1] The immediate danger of war came from Berlin, and an Anglo-French-Soviet alliance was " the only means to avert that danger ". But the instructions which he received from his Foreign Minister, M. Delbos, had a rather negative tendency: " France wants peace abroad

[1] *De Staline à Hitler. Souvenirs de deux ambassades, 1936–1939.* (Hachette.)

and at home, and the Franco-Soviet Pact of Mutual Assistance must not work in a contrary sense ". Therefore : " No preventive war " and " no Russian interference in our affairs " ; yet should war come, " what aid would the U.S.S.R. give us ? " Naturally France was anxious to avoid a new holocaust ; but

> when I was starting for Russia, I did not discern the deepest reason . . . why it was essential, crucial, for France to avoid war. Only toward the end of my stay in the U.S.S.R. did I become aware of it. . . . Vanquished, France would be Nazified ; victorious, she was bound, foremost owing to the destruction of German power, . . to sustain, with the rest of Europe, the crushing weight of the Slav world, armed with Communist flame-throwers.

The only chance lay in addressing oneself direct to Stalin. But no Ambassador could claim an interview with him, then only Secretary-General of the Communist Party : and Mr. Davies, the American Ambassador, was the only one he chose to see. M. Coulondre had to transact business with Litvinov, who was not even a member of the Politbureau. In spite of collisions and difficulties, Coulondre has retained a friendly feeling for him : " I am convinced that, like myself, he worked sincerely for a Franco-Soviet *entente* within the framework of the League of Nations ". In the very first interview Coulondre bluntly told Litvinov that unless the Russians strictly observed their promise not to meddle in French internal politics the Franco-Soviet Pact was dead. But the Russians complained of the Pact of Mutual Assistance having anyhow been put into cold storage.

> I knew only too well that the complaints were well-founded. Our technical departments had acted . . . with much levity. After having supplied the representatives of the Soviet armed forces with lists of war material available for them, they went back

> on most of their offers. The Admiralty vetoed the delivery of the promised naval guns, the War Office limited delivery of land guns to an old type.

Admiral Darlan was even unwilling to have a French Naval Attaché go to Moscow, lest a Soviet naval representative came to Paris; and while Gamelin "seemed desirous of receiving information concerning the development of the Soviet military strength . . . less objectivity was shown by his *entourage* in the study of the Russian problem". But Stalin

> is a realist . . . and cannot be bought off by words; he expects a Pact to yield returns. Yet he knew that this one was not doing so, because of the ill-feeling against the Soviets and their régime which abounded in France.

Coulondre himself had no illusions concerning the nature of that régime; of this his chapters on the U.S.S.R. are sufficient evidence.

> Through what a singular and terrible period my wife and I lived in the U.S.S.R. between 1936 and 1938! A life strange for a diplomatist, poignant for a human being, and disturbing for a historian.
>
> A strange life, that of a *bourgeois* at the heart of revolution and terror, where death continually claimed victims; he carrying on peacefully and acting safely in the midst of danger, protected by that very G.P.U. which struck down the others. A poignant life, for, so to say daily, men and women . . . with whom we had formed friendly relations, disappeared without our knowing where or why. A disturbing life, because of the need to preserve objectivity, when what I experienced, in spite of my isolation, wrenched my emotions of a man of the West.[1]

As the "purges" increased in severity M. and Mme Coulondre had to break off social relations, even of a

[1] Compare Coulondre's reactions to Soviet Russia with those of Dirksen; see above, pages 50-51.

completely unpolitical character: friendship bade them do so.

And yet all this was immaterial in the domain of international politics: what mattered was Russia's war potential and how it could be utilized to restrain Hitler. The conclusion which emerges from Coulondre's survey is that those who, from a loathing of the Bolsheviks or from fear of displeasing Hitler, refused to play the Russian card against him, cannot cite the present world position for their justification. The card they threw away was picked up by Hitler, and enabled him to bring on the war from which either the Nazis or the Bolsheviks were bound to emerge preponderant, no longer counterbalancing each other.

Coulondre emphasized in his reports to Paris that the question was not " whether the U.S.S.R. will, or will not, be with us, but *with whom* they will be ". Secret contacts had continued between Moscow and Berlin, though Coulondre believes that they snapped about the time of the Tukhachevsky trial, and were not resumed till after Munich. But to make the U.S.S.R. give up their ambiguous attitude, they would have had to be convinced " of our determination to oppose all aggression on the part of Hitler ". Coulondre was therefore anxious for military talks, which he knew " were expected by the Kremlin as evidence of our sincere intentions ". In April 1937, he went to Paris to forward the matter. There was resistance, notably from the General Staff, who feared that Russia might push France into a preventive war. Still, before returning to Moscow Coulondre received from the Quai d'Orsay a " highly interesting " top-secret draft for a preliminary military agreement. " I was never to hear of it again."

The weakness of the French Air Force was known to Coulondre, who, while in Paris, ascertained that Gamelin would have wished to obtain aircraft from Russia. A suitable fighter-plane was available. But as matters did not advance, Coulondre sent his Air Attaché, Major Donzeau, to Paris.

> On his return he informed me that the Air Ministry thought the airplane interesting technically, and yet told him to drop the matter, without giving their reasons.
>
> A few months later I talked to General Gamelin about it. "I supported Major Donzeau," he said, "but the service chief at the Air Ministry replied: 'Never such a humiliation'." "When an officer gives you such an answer, don't you put him under arrest?" I asked General Gamelin.

During the Czech crisis, at Coulondre's request the Military Attaché prepared a report on the Soviet Army, which Coulondre forwarded to the Quai d'Orsay. A few weeks later, the Attaché came to him rather crestfallen.

> In reply to his report he received from his department a letter containing a reprimand and rejecting his figures, with a sharp request to show greater moderation in his estimates of the Soviet military forces. . . . The letter was signed: "For the Minister, Dentz." (Condemned to death as a collaborator in 1945, which sentence was commuted to life-long imprisonment.)

"I have often asked myself", writes Coulondre, "why in 1938 the Russian factor was not correctly appreciated by the great majority of Frenchmen." The internal Russian crisis was one factor; another was the Polish illusion "which was to cost us dear".

> For the Polish trees people did not see the Russian wood. And they committed a twofold miscalculation: the first concerning the value of Poland as ally, disproved in 1938; and the second concerning the strength of her army, disproved in 1939.

A widespread dislike of the Bolsheviks, dating back to their defaults of 1917–1918, irritation at their interference in internal French politics, fear of Hitler, and the attitude of Great Britain, all worked in the same direction.

Czechoslovakia was the Allies' " last defensive position for saving peace " ; and March 1938 " was the decisive moment ". At that juncture Coulondre was again in Paris, and urged on Delbos that " if anything could make Soviet Russia emerge from her physical and moral isolation . . . it was Czechoslovakia ". After the *Anschluss* Litvinov proposed a conference to counter further German aggression ; and

> the Soviet Minister in Prague, while advising the Czechoslovak Government to show the greatest prudence and moderation toward Berlin, invited them " to seek, in conjunction with France, a concrete formula for military assistance to be rendered by the U.S.S.R. to Czechoslovakia ".

Once more Coulondre insisted on the imperative need of military talks with the U.S.S.R., now that " the Russian factor had attained maximum importance ".

Two changes of the French Government supervened in quick succession, in March-April 1938. Summoned to Paris by the new Foreign Minister, M. Bonnet, Coulondre saw him on May 20, the eve of the first Czech crisis. Bonnet professed to have been " very firm " in London ; and the upshot of his discourse was a suggestion of military talks with Russia. Coulondre joyfully concurred, but as Czechoslovakia was now in question he proposed to hold them between the three Powers in Moscow — though subsequently he somewhat modified his proposal : " to avoid undesirable reactions abroad " the talks were to be kept secret and to proceed separately, though parallel, between Czechs and French, Czechs and Russians, and Russians and French. But on May 23 Bonnet showed himself hesitant ; and so did Daladier, who wished for talks with the Russians and yet feared to annoy Hitler.

Coulondre continued to urge that Czechoslovakia was the line on which to bar Hitler's advance.

> As for Poland, I said . . . that we overrated her importance. Neither Russia, nor, as far as I could judge, Germany, considered her a front. For Hitler there were but two fronts, Russia and France. . . . I said it was a political absurdity to have conflicting Eastern alliances, and I thought the time had come to bring them into line by forcing Poland to declare colour. . . .
>
> M. Bonnet seemed to agree, and finally approved of opening talks.
>
> At the end of May I returned to Moscow thinking that at last a step forward had been taken. But the wind of fear was soon to sweep away, together with others, the page I had brought from Paris.

On July 1, Coulondre learnt, from a letter of the Czech Minister in Paris to his colleague in Moscow, that " for the present the French Government did not mean to engage in the proposed Franco-Soviet military talks in order not to upset the British Conservatives " (throughout that period a plausible excuse for shirking responsibilities or action).

In August 1938 Coulondre was once more in Paris: but this time he returned to Moscow with little hope for a Franco-Soviet alliance. " Still, it was my duty to do all I could to bring about a *rapprochement*, and to behave as if Paris desired it." But in Moscow, too, he was now up against a blank wall: it having become obvious that the Western Powers were unwilling to go to war over Czechoslovakia, the Soviet Government adopted an attitude of reserve to avoid compromising themselves towards Germany. As for the smaller nations, the Bulgarian Minister in Moscow said to Coulondre after Berchtesgaden that they would now all have " to toe the line with regard to Germany . . . to escape the fate which awaits Czechoslovakia ". And after Munich : " So it is true that France has abandoned Czechoslovakia, and with her us all, and with us her own age-long policy ". *Une déchéance*, Coulondre calls it.

> Yes, Munich tolled the knell of a France, the great France of yester-year and still of 1914, of the France which deep in our hearts we shall not cease to mourn. Oh! one must be chary of straining the meaning of words and facts. The bells that toll do not kill the sick man; they announce his death. Munich did not cause the fall of France, but recorded it. . . . And yet I do not think history will absolve the men who cravenly admitted the rearmament of Germany or the remilitarization of the Rhineland. They flouted our dead and sacrificed our children.

Nor will it absolve the makers of Munich.

When after the May crisis Poland was seen preparing to play the jackal to Germany (her alternative offer, whatever it was worth, was ignored and suppressed by Bonnet) Litvinov inquired of Coulondre what attitude France would adopt should Poland attack Czechoslovakia, and the U.S.S.R. in turn attack Poland; and he repeated the same question in Paris. The French replied that, as under the Czechoslovak-Soviet agreement the obligation to intervene only arose after France had done so, the answer was clear. But what " if for one reason or another the U.S.S.R. intervened though France did not budge? " retorted Litvinov. On September 23, with Poland massing troops against Czechoslovakia, Litvinov summoned the Polish Chargé d'Affaires at 4 A.M., and presented him with a Note threatening to denounce the Polish-Soviet Non-Aggression Treaty should the Poles cross the Czechoslovak frontier. But when on October 1 the Czechs submitted to the Polish ultimatum,

> " This is a new capitulation ", remarked bitterly Potemkin [Litvinov's deputy]. The annoyance he

> showed suggested that a Soviet intervention had been intended, but had been deprived of justification by the Czech decision.

A curious vista of might-have-beens opens when these moves are given their due weight. At the time their significance was overlooked by those who vastly overrated Poland's military strength and underrated Russia's; and it has not been reconsidered since. But it became obvious to Coulondre in his talks with Russian statesmen.

In Litvinov's absence, he saw Potemkin on October 4.

> He received me coldly and listened to me without a word. " I simply state the fact ", he said when I had finished, " that the Western Powers deliberately excluded the U.S.S.R. from the negotiations." A heavy silence ensued. Then emotion overcame him, and though a Slav and a diplomatist, he spoke out his mind: " My poor friend, what have you done? For us I see now no other way out except a Fourth Partition of Poland."
>
> It is singular that after this the Chancelleries should have dropped from the clouds when, ten months later, the German-Soviet Agreement supervened. Naturally I had informed Paris.

Coulondre quotes significant passages from his dispatches of October 4 and 18, 1938. Having summed up the Russian estimate of Munich as an abandonment of Eastern and Central Europe to the Germans, or even as an attempt to divert Hitler against the U.S.S.R., he writes:

> From France the Soviet Union expects nothing more at present; if it continues the Pact, it is not from any trust in its efficacy but as a reserve for the future, and perhaps also in order to save appearances, for in spite of the rodomontades of its rulers, it fears obvious isolation.
>
> In these circumstances, what remains to them

> except a return to the policy of an *entente* with Germany . . . ?[1]
>
> Undoubtedly in favouring a partition of Poland . . . Soviet Russia would . . . expose herself to direct contact with a country whose dynamism and military strength are superior to hers. . . .

Yet this would be the only form of German expansion to the East acceptable to Soviet Russia, and there was reason to suppose that the thoughts of her rulers were moving in that direction; and they inclined to think " that Paris will not show more solicitude for Cain than they had shown for Abel ".

> For my own part I reckon that were we to make a constructive policy with Poland, such as M. Beck spoke of to M. Noël [French Ambassador in Warsaw], and if consequently we were to confirm our alliance with that country, this could only be on condition that Great Britain gave to that policy the guarantee of her eventual armed support, and that Poland herself accepted the U.S.S.R. as covering Power (*comme puissance d'ados*). . . .
>
> My task is merely to supply your Excellency with data. I wish, however, to express the fervent hope that, if we still think it possible to intervene with a view to re-establishing a European order other than that dictated by Germany, our ground should this time be chosen with a clear view of the situation (*à bon escient*), that our commitments should not exceed our forces, and that our position should be sufficiently strong for us to maintain it to the end.

On October 16, Litvinov said to him in substance:

[1] I myself wrote on October 28, 1938, to my friend, Mr. Walter Elliot, then a Minister in the Chamberlain Cabinet: " I agree that Russia is not an easy problem, and there is much unclearness about her internal situation, her strength, and her foreign policy. But I do not think that either we or the French can be said to have handled her well before, during, or after the crisis; speeches by people in high and responsible positions decrying her value are not conducive to better relations or to active co-operation. And if we lose Russia, so much loss to us, and I am certain that Germany will, sooner or later, find her. L. B. N."

> "Henceforth the U.S.S.R. can merely watch from behind her own frontiers the extension of Germany's hegemony over Central and South-Eastern Europe. But should by any chance the Western Powers bethink themselves at last of arresting it, they will have to turn to us, for", he said with a pointed glance at me, "we shall have a word to say."

The time came when the Western Powers did "bethink themselves"; and "having failed to secure peace by working with Hitler, had to secure it against him". "This was the task to which they now applied themselves, but badly."

> The British Government went to work quickly, so quickly as to overshoot the mark. It suffices to look at the map in order to understand the gravity of the diplomatic situation thus brought about. Poland and Roumania formed a practically continuous front between the Baltic and the Black Sea separating Germany from the U.S.S.R. . . . Stalin had obtained, indirectly and without having to commit himself, that cover from the West which he had sought for 10 years. He was now on velvet: he could safely watch developments and carry on a double game in a way dear to the Russians. One should not tempt saints: still less those who are not saints. Besides, Hitler knew that on the day he attacked Poland an understanding with the U.S.S.R. was henceforth the only means to escape the two-front war which he feared.

The Western Powers, after having at Munich pushed Stalin towards Hitler, now pushed Hitler towards Stalin.

> Would it not have been better . . . to have turned frankly and sharply toward an Anglo-French-Russian alliance which Churchill, with his prophetic acumen, demanded, and which the Soviet Government was ready to make? There was no reason to fear that Beck would have subordinated himself to Hitler; the haughty pride of the Polish people would

> have prevented it. . . . After Poland's odious conduct toward Czechoslovakia, it would have been but just if she had had to pay the penalty and had to attempt, however painful the effort, a *rapprochement* with Soviet Russia.

The U.S.S.R. themselves offered to conclude an alliance with the Western Powers.

> That offer was almost more than could then be hoped for. I think it was made because the U.S.S.R. were still floating along their course toward the Western Powers, and because Litvinov, who had constituted himself the champion of collective security, was still head of their Foreign Office. . . . This chance came to us through Hitler's blunder of March 15: a passing chance which, if missed, does not return.

On November 21, 1938, Coulondre presented his credentials to Hitler.

> . . . of set purpose and contrary to my innermost convictions, I came to Berlin favourable to a revision of what might seem unacceptable to the German people in the demarcation of their Eastern frontiers, and resolved, so far as with me lay, to give Hitler " his chance ", if he really desired a peaceful organization of Europe.

And in the first address to the staff of his Embassy Coulondre said in substance:

> Munich is our starting point. Everyone is free to form his own judgment on the policy which brought us there. But the fact remains that the Western Powers went there to preserve peace. The question, the only question, with which we are faced now is whether peace can effectively be reached by that road.

The story of Coulondre's embassy in Berlin is told at length in the French *Yellow Book* of 1939: he spent (deducting nine weeks of absence) seven months in

Germany and these are covered by nearly one hundred of his published telegrams and dispatches, the most valuable material for that period that we had before the Nuremberg disclosures. The German chapters of his *Memoirs* should be read in conjunction with his official correspondence: they sketch in the background, add valuable detail, and weld his communications into a coherent whole. On some points his statements should also be compared with Bonnet's. Thus Bonnet writes in his memoirs about his talk with Ribbentrop on December 6, 1938:

> Next I very vigorously insisted . . . on Germany quickly giving her guarantee of Czechoslovakia's independence.

But M. Léger, Secretary-General of the Quai d'Orsay, told Coulondre:

> It was he, Léger, who raised the question of Czechoslovakia, recalling the promise given at Munich of a joint guarantee for that country, but Ribbentrop was evasive and M. G. Bonnet did not insist.

And next Bonnet writes:

> . . . on December 22, M. Coulondre, on instructions from me, made a *démarche* at the Wilhelmstrasse requesting that Germany give to Czechoslovakia the guarantee she had promised.

But Coulondre writes:

> . . . of my own initiative I made Czechoslovakia one of the principal points in my first talk with Herr von Weizsäcker, on December 22.

And when Weizsäcker suggested that the question of the guarantee had best be forgotten, Coulondre vigorously disputed the point.

> Having reported the conversation to M. G. Bonnet, I had to await his instructions before intervening once more. These reached me on February 5. . . .

After the extensive burning of the Quai d'Orsay archives in May-June 1940, and the German captures, the French have to collect their pre-war diplomatic documents from Embassies and enemy hiding-places; while some of the material which was only at the Quai d'Orsay can never be replaced. Hence the additional importance which attaches to French diplomatic memoirs, when reliable.

APPENDIX

GEORGES BONNET AS STATESMAN AND HISTORIAN

M. Bonnet, French Foreign Minister from April 1938 to September 1939, tells in his memoirs (which he extols as " an account free of errors or gaps ") how he had gone far and wide in search of help for Czechoslovakia, and how in the end France stood alone by her side; especially from Poland he claims to have met with nothing but blank refusals. Indeed, few could be found to defend Colonel Beck's miserable and short-sighted policy toward Czechoslovakia, and still less the way in which he finally enforced his demands against her. Yet, were Bonnet's negotiations with the Poles during the week which followed on the Czechoslovak mobilization of May 21, 1938, what he makes them in his unerring account?[1] The Polish side of the story has been given in a dispatch from M. Łukasiewicz, Polish Ambassador in Paris, printed by the Soviet Government from documents captured in Germany,[2] and in his article on " The Czechoslovak Problem in 1938 against the Background of Polish-French Relations ".[3]

Here are the outlines of Bonnet's story, as told in his memoirs. On May 22 a Note from Beck was communicated to him by Łukasiewicz starting with the sentence: " It is impossible for Poland to make a *démarche* in Berlin analogous

[1] See *Défense de la paix. De Washington au Quai d'Orsay*, pages 132-6.

[2] *Documents and Materials relating to the Eve of the Second World War*, vol. i, no. 11, pages 109-21. As published there, Łukasiewicz's dispatch bears the date of May 27, and refers to his interview with Bonnet as having taken place the same day: the correct date is May 26. But it will be seen in the photograph of the first page of Łukasiewicz's dispatch given in the Soviet publication, that the day of the month is added in ink: the Poles, like the French, used to leave the day blank in their typed texts to be filled in when the wire or report was dispatched. The copy captured by the Russians in Berlin was a carbon sent from the Paris Embassy to the Polish Embassy in Berlin; and, as Łukasiewicz has confirmed to me, the day was not written in by him, but by a clerk in the Chancellery who obviously inserted it the next day when sending it to the Berlin Embassy.

[3] In the quarterly *Sprawy Międzynarodowe*, vol. ii, nos. 2-3.

to that of Great Britain ". " About May 25 " (*vers le 25 mai*) Bonnet asked M. Noël, French Ambassador in Warsaw, to call on Beck — " *M. Léon Noël s'acquitta de sa mission avec fermeté* ". Bonnet saw again Łukasiewicz on May 25, and on May 27 sent further instructions to Noël in a wire which starts:

> While you had your talk with M. Beck, I received M. Łukasiewicz, and in spite of his evasive replies . . . pinned him down to the very clear questions I had previously put to him:
>
> 1. Will M. Beck stop in Berlin on his way to Stockholm? He replied in the negative. . . .

So much for Bonnet's account.

A Note starting, " It is impossible for Poland to make a *démarche* in Berlin analogous to that of Great Britain ", is clearly the answer to a request that she should. But the British *démarche* in Berlin was made late on May 21; Bonnet heard of it over the telephone from the French Embassy in London at night, while Sir Eric Phipps was with him; and the text of the instructions to Henderson for the *démarche* was communicated to the Quai d'Orsay about midnight.[1] It was therefore not till May 22 that Bonnet could have addressed the request to Poland to take action analogous to that of Great Britain; and the reply could not possibly have reached him the same day.

Noël saw Beck on May 22; on the 23rd, Beck left for Stockholm; passed through Berlin without breaking his journey; but gave to the Polish Ambassador in Berlin, M. Lipski, who travelled part of the way with him, the instructions to be sent to Łukasiewicz.[2] Beck did not return to Warsaw till the 30th at night. Hence instructions to Noël for a talk with Beck would hardly make sense on the 25th; nor could Bonnet have asked Łukasiewicz that day whether Beck, who had already arrived at Stockholm, would stop in Berlin on his way. A clear mishap for Bonnet the historian; the instructions which he claims to have sent to Noël " about

[1] See *Documents on British Foreign Policy, 1919–1939*, Third Series, vol. i, nos. 254, 256, and 266.

[2] This is the reason why in the first paragraph of Łukasiewicz's dispatch Beck's instructions of the 24th are referred to as " No. 8, Berlin ".

May 25 ", were presumably sent in the morning of the 22nd, and those dated by him May 27, were in fact sent in the morning of the 24th; the talk with Łukasiewicz referred to in that wire, is the talk of the 22nd ; while the note which Bonnet claims to have received on the 22nd, was in fact communicated to him on the 26th : a transposition of documents, of which Bonnet, the unerring historian, seems blissfully unaware.

His next error (*sit venia verbo*) is on the borderline between the realms of the historian and the statesman. Here is Beck's Note communicated to Bonnet by Łukasiewicz, and next, its text as printed by Bonnet in his memoirs.

Note communicated by Łukasiewicz

J'espère que le danger d'une agression directe allemande n'est pas d'actualité. Il est donc possible d'étudier la situation avec calme.

Le déclenchement d'un conflit plus vaste créerait évidemment une situation nouvelle par rapport à laquelle le Gouvernement polonais doit se réserver la possibilité d'un examen et d'une décision.

En ce qui concerne une démarche polonaise éventuelle à Berlin analogue à la démarche de la Grande-Bretagne, elle représenterait ipso facto l'acceptation par la Pologne d'avance d'une obligation unilatérale non prévue par les accords polono-français.

Je suis obligé de rappeler que dès le début des négociations franco-soviétiques, la Pologne a fait valoir ses réserves formelles à l'égard d'une collaboration quelle qu'elle soit en rapport avec cet accord et limitant son attitude envers la Russie au pacte de non-agression.

Les difficultés actuelles de la Tchécoslovaquie découlent, dans une grande mesure, de sa politique intérieure par rapport aux minorités. La minorité polonaise est brutalement maltraitée par les Tchèques. Je suis donc forcé de prévenir qu'une concession de Prague au bénéfice d'une minorité quelle qu'elle soit qui ne s'étendrait pas aux Polonais provoquerait immédiatement une tension entre la Pologne et la Tchécoslovaquie. Vu l'attitude actuelle du Gouvernement tchécoslovaque envers la minorité polonaise l'opinion publique polonaise n'approuverait aucune activité plus importante en faveur de la Tchécoslovaquie.

En confirmant, comme je l'ai fait le 7 mars, 1936, que nous sommes prêts à exécuter nos obligations d'alliance dans le cadre des accords existants et en affirmant que nous sommes prêts à une discussion amicale au sujet de tous nouveaux éléments de la situation (discussion basée sur la compréhension réciproque des intérêts de la Pologne et de la France) j'étais pourtant obligé de présenter les réserves susmentionnées.

Text as printed by Bonnet, page 132

Il est impossible à la Pologne de faire à Berlin une démarche analogue à celle de la Grande-Bretagne. Car cela représenterait l'acceptation par la Pologne d'une importante obligation non prévue par les accords polono-français. Dès le début des négociations franco-soviétiques, la Pologne a fait valoir ses réserves formelles à l'égard d'une collaboration, quelle qu'elle soit, en rapport avec cet accord et limitant son attitude envers la Russie au Pacte de non-agression. Les difficultés actuelles de la Tchécoslovaquie découlent, dans une large mesure, de sa politique intérieure par rapport aux minorités. La minorité polonaise est brutalement maltraitée par les Tchèques. Le gouvernement polonais prévient qu'une concession de Prague, au bénéfice d'une minorité quelle qu'elle soit, qui ne s'étendrait pas aux Polonais, provoquerait immédiatement une tension entre la Pologne et la Tchécoslovaquie.

This is not a mere, unavowed, summarizing of the text: it distorts the character and sense of the communication. From the phrase " elle représenterait *ipso facto* l'acceptation par la Pologne *d'avance* d'une obligation *unilatérale* " (paragraph 3 of the Note) the words here given in italics are, significantly omitted. With them the sentence suggests the possibility of Poland making such a declaration — for a *quid pro quo* previously agreed upon; from Bonnet's version all readiness to negotiate has vanished. That offer is explicitly restated in the concluding paragraph of the Note, again significantly deleted by Bonnet: " en affirmant que nous sommes prêts à une discussion amicale au sujet de tous nouveaux éléments de la situation (discussion basée sur la compréhension réciproque des intérêts de la Pologne et de la France). . . ." Beck's price might have proved excessive; there was never a trace of goodwill on his part towards Czechoslovakia; yet this communication was significant: hitherto the Poles had refused so much as to discuss with the French questions at issue between Poland and Czechoslovakia; now they offered to do so. On reading the instructions, writes Łukasiewicz, " I thought the French Government would feel encouraged to continue discussing with us Czechoslovakia with a view to effective co-operation ". But nothing of the kind happened.

The Polish offer, for what it was worth, was first torpedoed by Bonnet the statesman, and next obliterated by Bonnet the historian.

INDEX

INDEX

INDEX

THE END

PRINTED BY R. & R. CLARK, LTD., EDINBURGH